The Handmaid's Tale

by Margaret Atwood

Nicola Onyette

Series Editors:
Nicola Onyett and Luke McBratney

HODDER
EDUCATION
AN HACHETTE UK COMPANY

The publisher would like to thank the following for permission to reproduce copyright material:

Acknowledgments:

pp.vi: Susanne Becker: from *Margaret Atwood: Works and Impact*, ed. Reingard M. Nischik (House of Anansi Press, 2002); **pp.vii,3,5–6,28,36,37, 38,46–7,48,60,61,62,69: Margaret Atwood:** from *Writing with Intent: Essays, Reviews, Personal Prose 1983–2005* (Carroll and Graf, 2006); **pp.14,15, 16–17,20,23,24,25,26–7,28,29,30–1,32,33,34–5,39,40,41,42,43–4,45,46,48,52,53,58,63,67,69,71,72,81,95,96,97,98,99: Margaret Atwood:** from *The Handmaid's Tale* (Vintage, 1996); **p.35: Mervyn Rothstein:** from 'No Balm in Gilead for Margaret Atwood' from The New York Times (The New York Times, 17th February 1986), reproduced by permission of *The New York Times*; **p.38,67: Heidi Slettedahl Macpherson:** from *The Cambridge Introduction to Margaret Atwood* (Cambridge University Press, 2010); **pp.42,43: Linda Irvine:** from *Margaret Atwood: Works and Impact*, ed. Reingard M. Nischik (House of Anansi Press, 2002); **pp.43,51,76–7: Gina Wisker:** from *Atwood's The Handmaid's Tale: A Reader's Guide* (Continuum, 2010), © Gina Wisker, 2010, *Atwood's The Handmaid's Tale: A Reader's Guide*, Continuum used by permission of Bloomsbury Publishing Plc.; **pp.44,52–3,57: Barbara Hill Rigney**, from Women Writers: Margaret Atwood (1987, Palgrave Macmillan), reproduced by permission of Palgrave Macmillan; **pp.47,62: Margaret Atwood:** from 'Margaret Atwood: Rachel Carson's Silent Spring, 50 years on' from *The Guardian* (The Guardian, 7th December 2012), copyright Guardian News & Media Ltd 2016; **pp.50,67: Arthur Miller:** from *The Crucible* (Methuen Drama, 2010), reproduced by permission of The Wylie Agency, and from THE CRUCIBLE by Arthur Miller, copyright 1952, 1953, 1954, renewed © 1980, 1981, 1982 by Arthur Miller. Used by permission of Viking Books, an imprint of Penguin Publishing Group, a division of Penguin Random House LLC.; **p.50: Obituaries:** from 'Tammy Faye Messner' from *The Telegraph* (The Telegraph, 23rd July 2007), © Telegraph Media Group Limited 2007; **pp.52,60,61:** from *The Cambridge Companion to Margaret Atwood*, ed. Carol Ann Howells (Cambridge University Press, 2006); **p.52: Barbara Hill Rigney:** from *Margaret Atwood: Works and Impact*, ed. Reingard M. Nischik (House of Anansi Press, 2002); **p.53: Coral Ann Howells:** from *Margaret Atwood: Works and Impact*, ed. Reingard M. Nischik (House of Anansi Press, 2002); **pp.61,62: Gabriele Metzler:** from *Margaret Atwood's the Handmaid's Tale (Bloom's Modern Critical Interpretations)*, ed. Harold Bloom (Chelsea House Publications, 2001); **p.62: Joan Didion:** from 'The White Album' from *The White Album* (Farrar Straus Giroux, 2009); **p.62: Hermione Hoby:** from 'Margaret Atwood: interview' from *The Telegraph* (The Telegraph, 18th August 2013), © Telegraph Media Group Limited 2013; **pp.63,64: Madonne Miner:** from *Margaret Atwood's The Handmaid's Tale*, ed. Harold Bloom (Chelsea House Publications, 2001); p.76: David Staines: from *The Cambridge Companion to Margaret Atwood* (Cambridge University Press, 2006), reproduced by permission of Cambridge University Press; **p.77: Alison Flood:** from 'Margaret Atwood's new work will remain unseen for a century' from *The Guardian* (The Guardian, 5th September 2014), copyright Guardian News & Media Ltd 2016; **p.80: Terry Eagleton:** from *Marxism and Literary Criticism* (Routledge, 1976); **p.82: Julie Rivkin and Michael Ryan:** from *Literary Theory: An Anthology* (Wiley-Blackwell, 2004).

Every effort has been made to trace or contact all copyright holders, but if any have been inadvertently overlooked the Publishers will be pleased to make the necessary arrangements at the first opportunity.

Photo credits:

p.5 © The Granger Collection, NYC / TopFoto; **p.10** © hemantha_sl – Fotolia; **p.24** © Ronald Grant Archive / Topfoto; **p.27** © Trinity Mirror / Mirrorpix / Alamy; **p.32** © AF archive / Alamy; **p.42** Don O'Brien/https://www.flickr.com/photos/dok1/8371800030/sizes/o/ https://creativecommons.org/licenses/by/2.0; **p.43** © Claudio Divizia – Fotolia; **p.44** © Clive Barda / ArenaPAL / TopFoto; **p.48** public domain/ https://commons.wikimedia.org/wiki/File:Witchcraft_at_Salem_Village.jpg; **p.49** © AF archive / Alamy; **p.50** © ZUMA Press, Inc. / Alamy; **p.73** © Marta Iwanek/Toronto Star via Getty Images

Although every effort has been made to ensure that website addresses are correct at time of going to press, Hodder Education cannot be held responsible for the content of any website mentioned. It is sometimes possible to find a relocated web page by typing in the address of the home page for a website in the URL window of your browser.

Hachette UK's policy is to use papers that are natural, renewable and recyclable products and made from wood grown in well-managed forests and other controlled sources. The logging and manufacturing processes are expected to conform to the environmental regulations of the country of origin.

Orders: please contact Hachette UK Distribution, Hely Hutchinson Centre, Milton Road, Didcot, Oxfordshire, OX11 7HH. Telephone: +44 (0)1235 827827. Email: education@hachette.co.uk. Lines are open from 9 a.m. to 5 p.m., Monday to Friday. You can also order through our website: www.hoddereducation.co.uk.

© Nicola Onyett, 2016

First published in 2016 by

Hodder Education
An Hachette UK Company,
Carmelite House, 50 Victoria Embankment
London EC4Y 0DZ

Impression number   10 9 8 7 6

Year   2025 2024 2023 2022 2021

Cover photo (and throughout) © selimaksan/istockphoto

Typeset in 11/13pt Univers LT Std 47 Light Condensed by Integra Software Services Pvt. Ltd., Pondicherry, India

Printed and bound by CPI Group (UK) Ltd, Croydon, CR0 4YY

A catalogue record for this title is available from the British Library.

ISBN 978-1-4718-5410-1

Contents

Why read this guide?

The purposes of this A-level Literature Guide are to enable you to organise your thoughts and responses to the text, to deepen your understanding of key features and aspects, and to help you address the particular requirements of examination questions and non-exam assessment tasks in order to obtain the best possible grade. It will also prove useful to those of you writing an NEA piece on the text as it provides a number of summaries, lists, analyses and references to help with the content and construction of the assignment.

Note that above all else teachers and examiners are seeking evidence of an *informed personal response to the text*. A guide such as this can help you to understand the text, form your own opinions, and suggest areas to think about, but it cannot replace your own ideas and responses as an informed and autonomous reader.

How to make the most of this guide

You may find it useful to read sections of this guide when you need them, rather than reading it from start to finish. For example, you may find it helpful to read the 'Contexts' section before you start reading the text, or to read the 'Chapter summaries and commentaries' section in conjunction with the text – whether to back up your first reading of it at school or college or to help you revise. The sections relating to the Assessment Objectives will be especially useful in the weeks leading up to the exam.

NB: Line references in this guide refer to the 1996 Vintage edition of *The Handmaid's Tale*.

This guide is designed to help you to raise your achievement in your examination response to The *Handmaid's Tale*. It is intended for you to use throughout your AS/A-level English Literature course. It will help you when you are studying the novel for the first time and also during your revision.

The following features have been used throughout this guide to help you focus your understanding of the novel:

Context

`Context` boxes give contextual information that relates directly to particular aspects of the text.

TASK

Tasks are short and focused. They allow you to engage directly with a particular aspect of the text.

CRITICAL VIEW

Critical view boxes highlight a particular critical viewpoint that is relevant to an aspect of the main text. This allows you to develop the higher-level skills needed to come up with your own interpretation of a text.

Build critical skills

Broaden your thinking about the text by answering the questions in the **Build critical skills** boxes. These help you to consider your own opinions in order to develop your skills of criticism and analysis.

Taking it further ▶

Taking it further boxes suggest and provide further background or illuminating parallels to the text.

Top ten quotation

Top ten quotation

A cross-reference to Top ten quotations (see pages 97–100 of this guide), where each quotation is accompanied by a commentary that shows why it is important.

Context

The Handmaid's Tale is a dystopian vision set in the near future, after the overthrow of the government of the USA. Women's rights have been eroded with frightening speed as the new Republic of Gilead has restructured society according to an ultra-conservative social, cultural, religious and political framework. The narrator and central character, Offred, a powerless concubine or 'Handmaid', tells the story of her life within the household of Commander Fred and his wife Serena Joy. When reading the novel, you need to compare and contrast the contexts of production (i.e. the 1980s, when the novel was written) and reception (our contemporary world). Margaret Atwood has described dystopias as 'often more like dire warnings than satires, dark shadows cast by the present into the future. They are what will happen to us if we don't pull up our socks' (Atwood 2005: 94).

When *The Handmaid's Tale* was written, Atwood used the key cultural concerns of that time to construct her dystopian future, and some of her fears about women's rights, religious fundamentalism and the state of the planet have (fortunately) not come to pass – or not in North America, at any rate. Nevertheless, today's reader need only look at the position of women under extreme theocratic regimes such as that of the Taliban, the use of unethical and exploitative reproductive technologies and surrogacy arrangements, the widespread dissemination of violent hard-core pornography via the internet, the use of surveillance spyware to spy on a country's own citizens by major governments, the legally sanctioned persecution of gay men in some parts of Africa, and the impact of pollution and global warming to see that in some ways Atwood was startlingly prescient.

For many people today, *The Handmaid's Tale* offers not so much a glimpse of a possible terrible future as a reflection of a far more frightening present. As Susanne Becker has commented, 'this novel about a young woman forced to bear children under a totalitarian regime after a fundamentalist take-over in the US sparked great controversy and media attention … *The Handmaid's Tale* is also, in some ways, Atwood's strongest manifesto for freedom of the press – its abolition in the novel signifies an end to individual freedom and human rights. Atwood belongs to those writers of contemporary world literature who always address, both within and beyond their work, pressing global issues' (Becker, in Nischik 2000: 29). As the writer herself sees it, the dystopian genre she has chosen is as a form 'a way of trying things out on paper first to see whether we might like them, should we ever have the chance to put them into actual practice. In addition, it challenges us to re-examine what we understand by the word *human*, and above all what we intend by the word *freedom*' (Atwood 2005: 95).

The narrator of *The Handmaid's Tale* lives in the Republic of Gilead, a totalitarian theocracy that has overthrown the elected government of the USA. Because the birth rate has declined very sharply, the state has assumed control of the reproductive process and women are now banned from reading, voting, working or any other actions that might encourage them to challenge the power of the patriarchy. As the story begins, the narrator is living with a group of other trainee Handmaids in a converted gymnasium, which is now known as The Rachel and Leah Re-education Centre (or 'Red' Centre, for short). As time passes, the narrator describes her life as a Handmaid, in which her role is to give birth to a child for her high-ranking employers, Commander Fred and his wife, Serena Joy. The narrator is known by the patronymic 'Offred', literally 'of/Fred', which signifies her status as the Commander's possession.

Offred's narrative switches back and forth between descriptions of her cramped and restricted present life in the Commander's house while on her third and final assignment as a Handmaid, and vivid flashbacks to her previous life (including her time at the Red Centre, where the novel starts). She remembers her feminist mother, her loving husband Luke, their small daughter and her feisty best friend Moira. The reader discovers how the Gileadeans seized power via a military coup as a sinister backdrop of violence against women, environmental disaster and declining fertility led to the end of the American era. In her former life, Offred was a happy wife and mother who worked in a library, but when the Republic banned women from owning property or working, Offred, Luke and their little girl tried unsuccessfully to escape north across the border into Canada. She has not seen either of them since their capture.

With her marriage declared invalid because Luke had been married before, Offred is sent to the Red Centre. Older women known as Aunts train the Handmaids to be subservient concubines concerned solely with bearing healthy children. Offred is pleased to meet her old friend Moira at the Centre, but they lose touch again when Moira manages to escape.

Offred describes her routine, restricted and monotonous existence as the Commander's Handmaid in minute detail. She goes shopping with Ofglen, another Handmaid, and slowly the two women begin to form a bond. Together they visit the Wall outside what used to be Harvard University, where traitors to the Republic are hanged. They witness another Handmaid, Ofwarren, give birth to a baby girl. Offred also describes the Ceremony, during which the Commander has sex with her as she lies on top of Serena Joy. During a routine sexual health check, the doctor offers to get her pregnant, since the Commander may well be infertile; if this is true then Offred is in real danger, since a Handmaid who fails to get pregnant can be exiled and killed – but being 'unfaithful' to the Commander is an equally risky proposal.

As time goes on, Offred is asked to visit the Commander's study in secret at night. Against all the rules of the Gileadean theocracy, and behind the back of Serena Joy, they play Scrabble and she reads magazines. He asks her to kiss him and they begin to develop a more personal relationship, but Offred has still not become pregnant. As this is her third and last assignment, a terrible fate awaits should she fail to conceive this time: she will be labelled an Unwoman and exiled.

Desperate for a child, Serena Joy suggests that Offred has sex with the Commander's chauffeur, Nick, in the hope that the Handmaid will become pregnant and they will be able to pass off the baby as her husband's. Serena Joy bribes Offred with a photograph of the Handmaid's lost daughter, who was kidnapped after their failed escape attempt. The Commander secretly takes Offred to an illicit nightclub-cum-brothel called Jezebel's, where she meets Moira for the last time. Moira has chosen to work as a prostitute rather than be exiled to the Colonies, which is where those considered dangerous to the Gileadean regime are sent. That night the Commander and Offred have sex in a hotel room, ignoring the sanctity of the Ceremony and deceiving his wife.

Soon after they return home, Serena Joy orders Offred to visit Nick. Their secret sexual relationship develops into something stronger as she shares stories of her past life with him. As Offred's illicit personal relationship with Nick intensifies, the wider political situation in Gilead darkens ominously. Ofglen, who is a member of a rebel underground resistance movement trying to topple the theocratic regime, asks Offred to spy on the Commander. Offred and Ofglen attend a Salvaging (a public execution) followed by a Particicution, in which the women are encouraged to lynch a man accused of rape and effectively rip him to shreds. Ofglen rushes to strike the first blow, later telling Offred that the so-called rapist was in fact a member of the underground resistance and that she wanted to knock him unconscious to end his suffering.

When Offred goes shopping one morning, she is shocked to find that Ofglen has been replaced by another woman, who says that her predecessor committed suicide to escape the secret police. Meanwhile, the furious Serena Joy has found out about the Commander's secret relationship with Offred and has reported her to the authorities. Banished to her bedroom to await her fate, Offred sees a police van approaching the house. Nick says its occupants are actually members of the underground resistance who have come to save her; as Offred leaves with them, neither she nor the reader knows if Nick can be trusted – whether she is heading for freedom or imprisonment.

Offred's narrative ends here, but it is followed by an extra section called the 'Historical Notes'. In an epilogue dated June 2195, i.e. a couple of centuries after the collapse of the Gileadean regime, the noted Cambridge University anthropologist Professor Pieixoto is addressing an academic conference. He offers an analysis of Offred's story, which he and a colleague have transcribed and reconstructed from a bundle of old cassette tapes, explaining that no one will ever know whether the woman known as Offred did in fact escape to freedom. The last line of the novel, addressed to the audience gathered at the University of Denay, Nunavit by Professor Pieixoto, is deeply significant: '**Are there any questions?**'

Top ten quotation

Taking it further ▷▷

According to Margaret Atwood, 'All fictions begin with the question *What if…?* … there is always a *What if…?*, to which the novel is the answer. The *What if…?* for *The Handmaid's Tale* could be formulated: What if it *can* happen here? What kind of "it" would it be?' (Atwood 2005: 97–8). Discuss with the rest of your class the nature of the *What if…?* that drives the narrative within your other A-level texts.

Who's who in Gilead

Dystopian texts often explore the ways in which totalitarian regimes manipulate language, and Gilead's classification of its citizens into clearly defined and gendered groups perfectly exemplifies this. The distinct categories into which all Gileadeans are assigned are as follows:

Men

- ◥ **Commanders of the Faithful** – black-clad members of Gilead's ruling class who have extensive privileges.
- ◥ **Eyes** – spies and secret agents who enforce the Republic's laws.
- ◥ **Angels of Light** – soldiers who are accorded some respect and may marry.
- ◥ **Guardians of the Faithful** – lower-ranking soldiers who wear green uniforms and perform less-valued work; they may be of low intelligence, very young or very old. If they are lucky, the younger ones may become Angels.
- ◥ **Salvagers** – public executioners who wear black cloaks and hoods.
- ◥ **Gender Traitors** – gay men who are either killed outright or persecuted and sent to the Colonies. In exile they are forced to wear the same grey dresses as the Unwomen in an attempt to further humiliate and degrade them.

Women

- ◥ **Wives** are married to high-status men such as the Commanders. Their blue dresses reflect the traditional representation of the Madonna in Western art. When Wives become Widows they wear black, of course.
- ◥ **Daughters**, who wear virginal white robes, are the children of the Commanders and their Wives. Many have been adopted, since so many members of the Gileadean elite are infertile.
- ◥ **Handmaids** are fertile younger women who dress in red. They are used as surrogate mothers by elite childless couples.

Feminist critics would draw attention to the fact that while men in Gilead are accorded the respect of their rank or profession, women are defined and divided by their specific roles within a purely domestic or sexual context. This arbitrary and divisive situation encourages a climate in which women dislike, despise and fear each other.

- **Aunts** are older, unmarried and/or infertile women who monitor and control the Handmaids. Their robes are brown.

- **Marthas** are older women of low status who work as servants for the Gileadean elite. They dress in green. They are named after the biblical character who spent so long cleaning up before Jesus' visit to her house that she failed to listen to his teaching.

- **Econowives** are the legal wives of poorer men, and their multi-coloured striped robes indicate that their roles are multi-functional; their labour is not sub-divided but all-encompassing. This is because although poorer men were permitted to keep their 'legal' wives after the Gileadean coup, they are banned from having Marthas or Handmaids.

- **Unwomen** are 'difficult' types stigmatised as unfit to participate fully in Gileadean society. Comprising of feminists, lesbians, nuns, dissidents and the infertile, their fate is to be exiled. Handmaids who repeatedly fail to get pregnant become Unwomen. Dressed in grey, they haunt the dreaded Colonies like ghosts, cleaning up toxic waste.

- **Jezebels** are prostitutes and as such are allowed luxuries forbidden for all other women, such as make-up and alcohol. Often failed Handmaids, they have been sterilised. Instead of the colour-coded robes worn by other Gileadean women, the Jezebels dress in overtly 'sexy' costumes that predate the time of the Republic, such as cheerleader outfits and Playboy Bunny suits. Once their short careers are over, they are exiled to the Colonies.

Babies

- **Keepers** are healthy, normal newborns.

- **Unbabies**, colloquially known as **Shredders**, are the one in four Gileadean children born with defects, deformities or congenital abnormalities. They are subsequently done away with.

Target your thinking

- How does Atwood develop her themes, settings and characters as the narrative progresses? (**AO1**)
- What narrative methods does Atwood use to shape the reader's responses as the story unfolds? (**AO2**)

Dedications

Margaret Atwood dedicated *The Handmaid's Tale* to two significant people, Professor Perry Miller of Harvard University, who encouraged her to undertake research into the American Puritans, and her ancestor Mary Webster, who was hanged as a witch. Atwood credits Perry Miller with pointing out the extreme intolerant bigotry of Puritanism, noting that although the Puritans 'wanted the freedom to practise *their* religion … they were not particularly keen on anyone else practising his or hers' (Atwood 2005: 96). The so-called witch Mary Webster had an extraordinary escape from death, Atwood notes: 'they strung her up and let her dangle … [but] when they came to cut her down the next morning, she was still alive.' As the law does not allow for anyone to be punished twice for the same crime, Mary was then allowed to go free.

THE SALEM MARTYRS.

◀ Puritan witches being hanged at Salem, Massachusetts, in 1692

As Atwood comments wryly, 'I felt that if I was going to stick my neck out by writing this book, I'd better dedicate it to someone with a very tough neck' (Atwood 2005: 97). Atwood's conception of the theocratic Republic of Gilead is eerily reminiscent of the extreme religious intolerance of those very early Puritan settlers who persecuted the likes of Mary Webster, 'on the principle that no society ever strays completely far from its roots' (Atwood 2005: 97).

Epigraphs

Margaret Atwood has placed three introductory quotations before the beginning of *The Handmaid's Tale*. Each adds significantly to our understanding of her ideas and intentions.

Genesis 30:1–3

These verses from Genesis, the first book of the Old Testament, describe the jealous Rachel's solution to her inability to bear a child: asking her husband to use her servant, Bilhah, as a surrogate. According to the Bible, the twelve tribes of Israel are descended from the sons that the patriarch Jacob fathered with four different women: his two official wives, the sisters Leah and Rachel, and their two handmaids, Bilhah and Zilpah. This complex family network engenders the infamous sibling rivalry that emerges among Jacob's children, caused by his obvious preference for Joseph, the child that Rachel finally bears him.

Not only is this story used by the Gileadean theocracy to justify the use of Handmaids as surrogates for elite couples, it reminds us that in this totalitarian dictatorship, barrenness is always said to be the 'fault' of the wife as opposed to the husband. These Bible verses form the backbone of the Gileadean system of state-regulated reproduction and are used to legitimise the ways in which infertile women are devalued and degraded. They also inspire the name of the sinister 'Rachel and Leah Re-education Centre' that features in the novel, foreshadowing the ways in which the lowly Handmaids are taught to accept their inferior status and subservience to the official Wives.

As Atwood has noted, the Republic of Gilead, 'being derived from Puritanism, would, of course, need biblical sanction. Luckily for them, the Old Testament patriarch was notoriously polygamous; the text they chose as their cornerstone was the story of Rachel and Leah, the two wives of Jacob, and their baby competition. When they themselves ran out of babies, they pressed their handmaids into service and counted the babies as their own, thus providing a biblical justification for surrogate motherhood, should anyone need one' (Atwood 2005: 99).

Jonathan Swift's *A Modest Proposal* (1729)

A Modest Proposal is a shocking, despairing and vicious satirical pamphlet by Jonathan Swift, the author of *Gulliver's Travels*, in response to the terrible poverty existing in Ireland at the time of writing. Swift offers what he terms a 'modest proposal' (i.e. a humble suggestion) for saving hordes of Irish babies and children from starvation by cooking and eating them instead, offering a range of tempting recipe options, such as boiling, frying, baking and fricasséeing. In suggesting that the problem of the desperately poor having children they cannot afford can be solved simply by selling off surplus babies for food, Swift presents his apparently insane scheme of state-sponsored cannibalism to an implied audience that might well take the idea seriously. In quoting this master satirist, Atwood signposts her intention to hold up a mirror to the serious social problems she has identified within her own contemporary cultural context.

Sufi proverb

This proverb suggests two key ideas that underpin *The Handmaid's Tale*: firstly, that under extreme conditions the human survival instinct is extremely strong, and secondly that the state doesn't need to involve itself in regulating every aspect of its citizens' private lives, since legislating against the obvious is self-evidently pointless. Atwood implies that no totalitarian regime can ever really destroy our essential humanity, and that the Gileadean regime's creepy micromanagement of its citizens' lives is completely unwarranted.

Section I Night: Chapter 1

Chapter 1: The Rachel and Leah Re-education Centre

The female narrator of *The Handmaid's Tale*, later identified (in Chapter 24) as bearing the name Offred, lives with a group of other women in what was once a gymnasium on the campus of Harvard University and is now known as The Rachel and Leah Re-education Centre, or 'Red' Centre for short. They are being supervised by two older women known as Aunts and are guarded by the Angels, soldiers of the Gileadean army. Offred thinks about the fun times that would have been enjoyed by the students who attended Harvard in the days before the Republic of Gilead overthrew the American government. She secretly exchanges names with the other trainee Handmaids.

Commentary The first of the seven 'Night' interpolations that split up the main (by implication 'daytime') sections of the text, this short section is typical of the way in which Offred retreats from her nightmare reality into memories of the past. Her private thoughts and desires suggest her refusal to allow herself to be fully subjugated by the Gileadean regime, despite the many restrictions placed upon them. Five young women are listed at the end of this section – Alma, Janine, Dolores, Moira and June. By the end of the novel, each of them has been identified within the context of the Gileadean regime – Janine, for example, becomes the Handmaid known as Ofwarren – with the exception of the last. Thus it may be that June is the narrator, Offred, herself, for once visible beneath the shadow of her demeaning patronymic.

> **Context**
>
> Sufism is a mystical Islamic-based religion whose followers believe that people should try to find God purely as an act of love, seeking to repent of their sins and be of good character as they go about their daily lives.

> **Context**
>
> Founded in 1636 in Cambridge, Massachusetts, Harvard is one of the most famous and well-respected universities in the world. In the USA, Yale and Harvard enjoy the same super-elite reputation and status that the universities of Oxford and Cambridge have in the UK. Margaret Atwood did postgraduate study at Harvard in the 1960s.

CRITICAL VIEW

The narrator is known as Offred because she is the concubine 'of/Fred'. Commander Warren's Handmaid is, similarly, known as Ofwarren, and Commander Glen's as Ofglen. Many women do not to take their husband's surname upon marriage, suggesting a wish to resist having their identity subsumed into that of another person and a recognition that names are symbolic markers of one's personal and social identity. Yet most women bear surnames passed on by a man – their father – anyway, and as Shakespeare's Juliet once asked, 'What's in a name? that which we call a rose / By any other name would smell as sweet.' How might feminist critics interpret patterns of naming in *The Handmaid's Tale*?

TASK

In 1963 writer Hannah Arendt witnessed the trial of the high-ranking Nazi Adolf Eichmann for crimes against humanity, following his involvement in the mass deportation of Jews to the concentration camps during the Second World War. Arendt coined the phrase 'the banality of evil' to suggest that rather than being a madman or psychopath, Eichmann was an unimaginative man motivated less by a fanatical devotion to the Nazi cause than by a dull determination simply to obey orders. How far does Arendt's phrase apply to the ironically named Aunts, who brainwash the Handmaids under orders from above?

Section II Shopping: Chapters 2–6

Chapter 2: The Commander's household

Unlike Chapter 1, which was narrated in the past tense, Offred now describes her bare, bleak room within the Commander's house in the present. She explains the crucial importance of dress in identifying the various groups of Gileadean women. As a Handmaid, Offred wears a distinctive red costume with white wings that shield her face, while the Marthas – Rita the cook and Cora the maid – wear green uniforms. Offred prepares to go shopping and Rita gives her the tokens that will allow her to buy eggs, cheese and meat.

Commentary There is envy and jealousy among the women of the household and, while the lonely Offred wishes she could communicate with the Marthas, relationships between different groups of women are discouraged. The kitchen gossip she overhears suggests that there is substantial mistrust and dislike among the women of Gilead, with one jealous Wife stabbing a Handmaid with a knitting needle.

Chapter 3: Serena Joy

This chapter focuses upon the Commander's privileged Wife, Serena Joy. This is Offred's third assignment as a Handmaid and while she had hoped that Serena

Joy would be an improvement on one of the previous Wives she had worked for, who was apparently an alcoholic, Commander Fred's Wife is in fact unfriendly and aggressive, warning Offred against any idea of becoming a potential rival for her husband's affections. Offred realises that Serena Joy was once a famous singer on the Growing Souls Gospel Hour, a religious television programme that Offred used to watch as a child.

Commentary Serena Joy, who must be some fifteen to twenty years older than Offred, is bitter and resentful. Stigmatised as sterile (since in Gilead infertility is always taken to be the Wife's fault), she has to put up with the humiliation of allowing another woman to bear the Commander's child. The hypocrisy and unfairness of a regime in which the elite impose laws upon others that they themselves then flout is signalled when she smokes in front of Offred; the Handmaids are, unsurprisingly, not allowed alcohol, coffee or cigarettes. Yet in spite of (or, of course, because of) having the Marthas to do all her work and a Handmaid to bear her children, Serena Joy has all the satisfaction of having helped to dig a pit into which she herself has fallen headfirst.

Taking it further ▶▶

The lives of the Commanders' Wives parody those of the stereotypical submissive 'Angel in the House' immortalised in Coventry Patmore's famous Victorian poem; indeed their role is encapsulated in the line, 'Man must be pleased; but him to please / Is woman's pleasure'. Do an internet search for the text of this poem, and see if you can find any other phrases or ideas that reflect the idealised wifely role Serena Joy seems to find so difficult to manage.

> **Context**
>
> The trope of the eternal triangle is a staple within the literature of love, providing rich opportunities for a writer to explore the darker side of human relationships, where adultery, jealousy and pain coexist.

Chapter 4: Offred and Ofglen go shopping

Offred and her fellow Handmaid Ofglen meet up in order to go shopping, as they are forbidden to leave the house unaccompanied. They speak carefully, unsure how far they can trust each other, before passing through a security checkpoint into town.

Commentary Paranoia mixed with the normal sexual impulses of an attractive young woman starved of all normal outlets for her affections is seen in this chapter, as Offred notices Nick for the first time and sees one of the Guardians at the checkpoint literally 'checking her out'.

Chapter 5: Offred and Ofglen are shopping; Ofwarren is pregnant

Offred remembers how different life was for women before the overthrow of the American government, when women were subject to petty sexual harassment. Now, no man would dare talk to a woman on the street, let alone wolf-whistle at her. When some Japanese tourists ask if they can take pictures of the Handmaids, they decline for fear of appearing immodest in front of the tour guides, who may well be Eyes. Offred recognises a very pregnant Janine, now renamed Ofwarren.

Commentary Significantly, Ofglen does not answer when the tourists ask if she is happy, so it is Offred who says that yes, they are. Given the Victorian levels of extreme modesty imposed upon the Handmaids, Offred thinks that Janine/Ofwarren has gone out shopping purely to advertise her success in becoming pregnant.

TASK

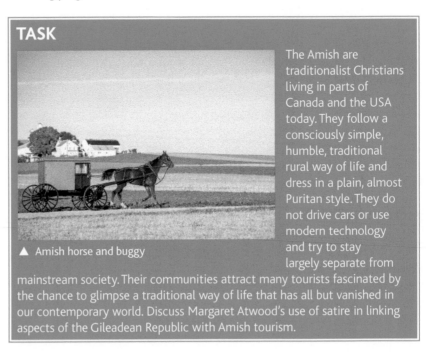

▲ Amish horse and buggy

The Amish are traditionalist Christians living in parts of Canada and the USA today. They follow a consciously simple, humble, traditional rural way of life and dress in a plain, almost Puritan style. They do not drive cars or use modern technology and try to stay largely separate from mainstream society. Their communities attract many tourists fascinated by the chance to glimpse a traditional way of life that has all but vanished in our contemporary world. Discuss Margaret Atwood's use of satire in linking aspects of the Gileadean Republic with Amish tourism.

Chapter 6: Offred and Ofglen pass the church and the Wall

The Handmaids pass a former Puritan church that is now preserved as a museum. Facing the church is the Wall, where the corpses of traitors to the regime are exhibited. The six dead bodies currently on display are those of doctors who had performed legal abortions in pre-Gileadean times; they have now been executed for 'crimes' committed in the past. In a society in which fertility and reproduction are of utmost importance, terminating a pregnancy is seen as the absolute essence of evil.

Commentary The preservation of the Puritan church symbolises the extent to which the Gileadean regime seems to fetishise aspects of that historically repressive religious regime. It is worth remembering that Margaret Atwood dedicated *The Handmaid's Tale* to Professor Perry Miller, who opened her eyes to the true nature of the Puritan theocracy by pointing out that their aim in coming to America was to enforce their own version of extreme Protestantism on others.

Context

The US Supreme Court decision in the landmark *Roe vs Wade* case (1973) enforced a woman's right to have an abortion up to the point when a foetus might be viable outside the womb. It overturned many existing legal restrictions on abortion in the US. This iconic example of the hard-won reproductive rights achieved by first-wave feminists would have been one of the first pieces of existing legislation thrown out by the Gileadean theocracy, for being anathema to its moral values.

Section III Night: Chapter 7

Chapter 7: Offred remembers: Moira, her daughter and her mother

Offred remembers her friend Moira and their days at university; she also remembers walking in the park as a little girl along with her feminist mother, and being informed by the Gileadean authorities that her daughter was being taken away from her to be raised by a more suitable parent. Time and memory seem fragile and unstable for Offred, who suspects she was drugged before her daughter was kidnapped. She recalls a photograph of her child hand-in-hand with a stranger. The reader presumes that this is an infertile Wife who has now adopted her.

Commentary This chapter shows how hard it is to recapture the past. Offred invents an imaginary audience for her oral narrative in order to tell the tale she is forbidden to write down. Her childhood memory of seeing a public bonfire of pornographic magazines reminds us of the dangers of censorship, while the fragmented story of how Offred lost her child is clearly something so traumatic that as yet she cannot process it. The irony of both radical feminists and extreme religious conservatives wanting to ban pornography suggests that all attempts to manage, control and supervise female sexuality may be seen as suspect.

Section IV Waiting room: Chapters 8–12

Chapter 8: Life in Gilead

Offred and Ofglen see three new bodies on the Wall and pass a group of Econowives who are antagonistic towards them. At home, Offred thinks about how Serena Joy's life has changed. After her television career ended, she became a well-known advocate for traditional conservative family values, urging women not to work outside the home. Now that the very situation she advocated has come to pass, she is as trapped and confined as is Offred herself. As Offred goes to her room, the Commander nods to acknowledge her presence, which is a small but significant breach of the rules.

Commentary The Econowives' hostility is another reminder of the way Gileadean society divides women and alienates them from each other. Her essential powerlessness as a female – even one of the highest status – causes Serena Joy to bully and harass the women she outranks.

Chapter 9: Offred remembers Luke and imagines the life of her predecessor

Top ten quotation

Offred remembers her ordinary, happy life with her husband Luke before her mind wanders back to her arrival at the Commander's house. She has discovered a Latin phrase written inside her wardrobe – *nolite te bastardes carborundorum* – but cannot translate it. She imagines that this is a secret message left for her by the Commander's previous Handmaid, who would also, like her, have borne the patronymic 'Offred'. Rita the cook informs her that she is the latest in a line of Handmaids.

Commentary This mysterious Latin phrase encapsulates the former Offred's determined battle to resist the Gileadean regime. Its meaning is revealed by the Commander only in Chapter 29.

Chapter 10: Offred remembers: women's lives before the fall of America

Time is passing. As Offred sings to herself in her room to evoke the freedom of pre-Gileadean times, she is indulging in a seemingly harmless pastime, which is nevertheless now forbidden by the regime. She remembers her college days with affection, thinking back to her friend Moira's ironic feminist 'underwhore' party, when she sold sexy lingerie, and when she sees Nick driving the Commander away from the house, she thinks back to the time she and Moira lobbed water bombs out of their bedroom windows. She also recalls reading newspaper reports about violence against women; the only word she can read now is 'faith', which has been embroidered on a cushion in her bedroom.

Commentary The startling contrasts between Offred's past and present are powerfully evoked in this chapter. Once a working wife and mother herself, the sight of Commander Fred being driven off to work by his male chauffeur grates on her nerves. The Christian virtues of faith, hope and charity are often linked together, since they derive from the Bible passage 'And now abideth faith, hope, charity, these three: but the greatest of these is charity' (1 Corinthians 13:13). 'There must have been three, once,' Offred realises, 'HOPE and CHARITY, where have they been stowed?' (Atwood 1996: 119). The symbolism inherent in the disappearance of the cushions embroidered with 'hope' and 'charity' is starkly clear; they have vanished from Gilead, along with the virtues they represent. Reflecting on her position in the Gileadean regime, Offred comments: '**We were the people who were not in the papers. We lived in the blank white spaces on the edges of print.**' Her story is not valued enough to be told, and is not even allowed to be told. Through this Atwood reminds us to remember the untold stories, disallowed by the literary narrative.

Context

Women are currently banned from driving in Saudi Arabia. In 2013, in response to a growing protest movement that aimed to reverse the ban, the prominent Saudi religious leader Sheikh Saleh Al-Loheidan warned that women who drive cars risk damaging themselves and may give birth to deformed children. His remarks immediately went viral on the internet and were widely challenged.

Top ten quotation

Taking it further ▶

Offred chooses to sing snatches from two exceptionally famous American songs, the gospel hymn *Amazing Grace* and Elvis Presley's 1956 hit *Heartbreak Hotel*. Do an internet search for the lyrics of these two iconic ballads and think about why Margaret Atwood has chosen them to reflect aspects of Offred's plight.

Chapter 11: Offred visits the doctor

Offred goes for her monthly medical check-up. Normally the doctor examines her without looking her in the face or speaking to her any more than is strictly necessary. This time, however, he not only suggests that the Commander could well be sterile, but also that he (the doctor) could have sex with Offred to ensure she has a child. This conversation is very risky, as officially all infertility is down to barren *women*. Knowing that to be caught out in a deception of this kind would mean death for both of them, Offred declines.

Commentary This short chapter, as well as stressing the commodification of women's bodies that is such a central theme of the text, also poses the central dilemma of who can be trusted when one is living in a climate of deadly fear. If the doctor were to report that Offred had failed her medical examination, she would be exiled to the Colonies to pick over nuclear waste. As a result, the doctor can be as sexually predatory as the Commander, trading security for sex.

Chapter 12: Offred takes a bath

Offred lies in the bath, looking in wordless wonder at her own naked body. She recalls a disturbed woman who once tried to kidnap her daughter when they were out shopping. It seems that three years have passed since Offred's five-year-old child was taken from her. The fact that she must bathe before having sex with the Commander reminds us that in Gilead, sex is seen as sinful.

Commentary The fact that a desperate childless woman once tried to kidnap Offred's daughter foreshadows the state-approved theft of her child under the Gileadean rules. The description of Offred bathing before she has sex with the Commander can be seen as a grotesquely parodic description of a woman excitedly preparing for a date with the man she loves. '**My self is a thing I must now compose, as one composes a speech**.' The way that Offred must behave is not natural to her but is something she has been taught: it is forced not organic.

Section V Nap: Chapter 13

Chapter 13: Offred remembers: Janine's rape, Moira's resistance and her own failed escape

Offred remembers two incidents at the Red Centre involving the diametrically opposed characters of Moira and Janine. Whereas Moira boldly resisted the Aunts' attempts to indoctrinate her, Janine (i.e. the pregnant Ofwarren) crumbled under the

Taking it further ▶

Ian McEwan's novel *The Child in Time* (1987) tells the story of writer Stephen Lewis, whose three-year-old daughter Kate is kidnapped during a trip to the supermarket. It deals with the traumatic impact of Kate's disappearance, the gulf that opens up between Stephen and his wife, Julie, and how they come to accept that Kate is lost forever. You might enjoy comparing this novel with *The Handmaid's Tale.*

Top ten quotation

Taking it further ▶

The 1991 Chinese film *Raise the Red Lantern* tells the story of Song Lian, who becomes the Fourth Mistress (concubine) of a wealthy warlord. It brilliantly dramatises the jealous rivalry that exists between the women of the household as they compete for the favour of their master. You might consider the extent to which the old saying 'divide and conquer' is highly appropriate to both this film and *The Handmaid's Tale*.

intense pressure and testified to having been gang-raped at the age of just fourteen. Offred views her body differently now, feeling that whereas it used to give her pleasure, she is now no more than a walking womb. She has a flashback to the night her family was captured when trying to escape across the Canadian border to safety.

Commentary When, with Aunt Lydia's encouragement, the other trainee Handmaids accept the horrifying idea that Janine *deserved* to be gang-raped because of her 'sinful' flirting, we see further evidence of the frightening 'women beware women' culture that exists in Gilead. This chapter provides further evidence that the pressures of living within a viciously oppressive patriarchal culture turn women against each other, as the castigation of her peers forces Janine to admit that the rape was indeed her own fault. When Offred describes how the other Handmaids actually enjoyed bullying and abusing Janine, we recognise just how distorted female relationships have become; 'We meant it, which was the bad part' (Atwood 1996: 82).

Section VI Household: Chapters 14–17

Chapter 14: The household prepares for the Ceremony

The entire household assembles for the ritualistic Ceremony and watches the television news while awaiting the arrival of the Commander. The news reports suggest the paranoia engendered by the Gileadean regime, which is always summoning up ideas of rebellion to inculcate fear among its people. Offred's mind drifts off to the plans she and Luke made for their escape.

Commentary The Commander's persistent lateness suggests that his heart is not really in the Ceremony. The fact that we read in this chapter about Offred's plans for escape *after* reading about the plan's failure in the previous chapter shows how fuzzy and non-linear her memories have become.

Chapter 15: The Commander reads from the Bible

The Commander reads Bible passages about childbearing, such as the story of Rachel and Leah from the book of Genesis. Offred recalls how this tale was central to her experiences at the Red Centre. She thinks of how Moira faked an illness as part of a daring escape plan.

Commentary The Bible is kept under lock and key, symbolising how the word of God is available now only as interpreted by the Commander, who represents the powerful male elite who use it to justify their behaviour. As well as using the Bible to legitimise the role of the Handmaids, of course, the regime also quotes scripture to uphold its racist ideology; the news reports reveal how black people have been labelled as the descendants of Noah's despised and rejected son Ham in order to separate them from other races. Offred's flashbacks reflect the many roles she once fulfilled in her busy past life (wife, daughter, mother and friend) and that are now denied her as Commander Fred's concubine.

Chapter 16: The Ceremony

The culmination of the Ceremony entails the Commander having sex with Offred while she lies between Serena Joy's legs. Offred rests her head on Serena's pubic bone and the two women hold hands. Serena Joy gets rid of Offred as soon as the Commander leaves the room, despite the rules stating that the Handmaid should rest for ten minutes following the Ceremony in order to maximise her chances of getting pregnant.

Commentary This, probably the most iconic chapter in the novel, memorably captures one of Atwood's major themes – the exploitation and abuse of the female body as a way of subjugating women. The Ceremony is both hideous and humorous; after all the high-falutin religiosity of the run-up to the great event, the sexual act itself is as impersonal as artificial insemination. The Commander is mechanically 'fucking … the lower half' of Offred's body, while she tries her best to ignore what is happening. Of the three participants, it's Serena Joy who most loathes the situation. As Serena Joy 'l[ies] on the bed, gazing up at the canopy above her, stiff and straight as an effigy', Offred wonders 'Which of us is it worse for, her or me?' (Atwood 1996: 104; 106).

Context

Offred's reference to Queen Victoria's advice to her daughter about enduring marital sex - 'lie back and think of England' - is somewhat misleading, as there is considerable evidence to suggest that the Queen very much enjoyed a healthy sex life with Prince Albert. What she disliked was what she referred to as 'die Schattenseite', or the 'shadowside' of marriage - that is, being semi-permanently pregnant and having to endure the agony of childbirth.

Chapter 17: Breaking the rules

Offred uses some stolen butter to moisturise her skin, humorously describing buttering herself 'like a piece of toast'. Restlessly she decides to sneak downstairs and steal a dried-up daffodil from one of Serena Joy's vases to forge another link in a chain of hidden messages; she wants to press it and leave it for the Commander's next Handmaid to find. To her shock she meets Nick in the darkened room and they kiss passionately. Nick gives Offred the message that the Commander wants to see her alone.

Commentary This chapter, positioned as it is directly after the blacker-than-black comedy of the Ceremony, is one in which everyone seems intent on breaking the rules. From stealing butter to use as a body balm, Offred progresses to sneaking out of her room to perform a small but highly significant act of defiance in taking a flower and giving it another meaning entirely. Her intimate encounter with Nick is equally dangerous for them both, but most surprising of all is the rebellion of Commander Fred himself, who seems intent on defying the sexual rules of the society that has afforded him such privileged high status.

Section VII Night: Chapter 18

Chapter 18: Offred remembers: her husband Luke

Having just kissed Nick, Offred remembers Luke in different ways: as making love to her while she was pregnant with their daughter, as lying dead after their failed escape or in prison or and as having successfully crossed the border into Canada.

Commentary Luke is becoming less real to her as Nick begins to play a larger role in her life, but Offred's desperate attempt to keep his memory alive suggests the importance of hope as a way of surviving terror. We are reminded once more of the three Christian graces – faith, hope and charity – and that Gilead affords space only for 'blind faith'.

Section VIII Birth Day: Chapters 19–23

Chapter 19: The Handmaids witness Ofwarren give birth

A red van (Birthmobile) collects Offred and her fellow Handmaids to attend the birth of a baby. The mother is 'Ofwarren, formerly that whiny bitch Janine', as Offred notes (Atwood 1996: 125). The fear is that the child may be born with abnormalities as a result of the environmental pollution that devastated the USA before the Gileadean coup, although Commander Warren and his Wife had checked her pedigree carefully: 'A strong girl, good muscles. No Agent Orange in her family' (Atwood 1996: 125). Offred thinks back to Aunt Lydia's lessons on the need for the Handmaids to reproduce and her castigation of women who could not or would not bear children. While in pre-Gileadean times, women had access to pain relief in childbirth, this is now banned because, it is argued, God wants women to suffer. The Wives turn up in a separate Birthmobile and once more we see the vast and unbridgeable gulf between two opposing groups of women.

Commentary Offred's description of the series of man-made disasters that paved the way for the Gileadean coup goes hand-in-hand with her concerns about the health of Ofwarren's soon-to-be-born baby. We hear how the 'air got too full, once, of chemicals, rays, radiation, the water swarmed with toxic molecules' and how eventually 'they creep into your body, camp out in your fatty cells. Who knows, your very flesh may be polluted, dirty as an oily beach, sure death to shore birds and unborn babies' (Atwood 1996: 122). Due to the never-named environmental catastrophe that brought about the downfall of the USA and the unknown effects on the health of those who lived through it, the Birth Day may not signal a celebration of new life but a wake. As Offred worries, 'What will Ofwarren give birth to? A baby, as we all hope? Or something else, an Unbaby, with a pinhead or a snout like a dog's, or two bodies, or a hole in its heart or no arms, or webbed hands and feet? There's no telling' (Atwood 1996: 122).

Chapter 20: Ofwarren is in labour; Offred remembers her mother

In an even more grotesque parody of the already grotesquely parodic Ceremony, as Ofwarren labours in agony, Commander Warren's Wife lies in another room as if she is herself is in the process of giving birth. Offred remembers her indoctrination at the Red Centre, in which the Aunts used hard-core violent porn to prove to the Handmaids that women need to be protected against men. She also recalls seeing an old newsreel film aimed at undermining Unwomen (i.e. feminists), which actually featured her own mother at a protest rally.

Commentary Offred's mother symbolises the first wave of early feminists who fought many of the key battles for equality and reproductive rights that later generations of women came to take for granted. The warning is clear; as Offred reflects, the clock can be – and in Gilead clearly has been – turned back. Aunt Lydia's lessons revive the feminist argument that pornography objectifies women and presents them as enjoying sexual violence or degradation. But in Gilead, rather than contest the causes of violence against women, the system ostensibly protects them from it by veiling and cloistering them. To an extent, this extreme repression works; when Offred and Ofglen go shopping they are kept 'safe' by the checkpoint Guardians. But, Atwood surely invites us to ask, where do we draw the line between the Commander's legitimised 'fucking' and the classic nightmare rape attack by a nameless stranger in the street?

Chapter 21: Ofwarren gives birth

The Handmaids chant as Ofwarren gives birth. Once more, the surrogacy element of the Handmaid's role is emphasised as Commander Warren's Wife sits on the Birthing Stool above Ofwarren. Once the baby is born, the Wife climbs into bed, cuddles 'her' new daughter and chooses the name Angela. Now that Ofwarren has fulfilled her sacred duty as a Handmaid, she cannot now be labelled an Unwoman or exiled.

Commentary The birth of Ofwarren's baby is a curiously old-fashioned female-dominated community event that seems to reflect the arcane rituals of some long-lost ancient pre-industrial society. The highly technological and medicalised births many women experience today are presented as a thing of the past, but in the absence of any kind of prenatal testing, the fear of producing an Unbaby looms large.

Chapter 22: Moira's escape

Offred remembers Moira's Houdini-like escape from the Red Centre, which involved taking Aunt Elizabeth hostage and hijacking her security pass, before waltzing out right under the noses of the guards.

Context

In another example of the importance of naming in the text, the forename 'Angela' comes from the Greek word 'angelus', meaning 'messenger of God'. It seems clear that Commander Warren's Wife has chosen this symbolic name to express her pious belief that the child has been created in a holy way and is a living endorsement of the Gileadean surrogacy policy. The fact that Angela turns out to be an Unbaby – a Shredder – gives the lie to this comforting idea.

Commentary Moira is for many readers the true heroine of *The Handmaid's Tale* – the only character who dares to openly challenge the regime. A witty, daring, street-smart improviser, Moira's theft of Aunt Elizabeth's uniform and security pass is a highly symbolic act of resistance. When we meet her later, wearing a very different uniform, Atwood is inviting us to compare Moira's use of costumes to cloak and obscure her identity.

Chapter 23: Offred visits the Commander in secret

Offred goes to the Commander's study, aware that if Serena Joy were to discover such a serious breach of the rules she could have her declared an Unwoman and exiled, but she is powerless to defy the Commander. Rather than being forced to submit to rape, however, the Commander asks her to play the old-fashioned word game Scrabble. As this involves reading, it is completely against the rules. The Commander asks her to kiss him and when she does so, he remarks sadly that he had hoped she would kiss him as if she really meant it.

Commentary The Commander, as trapped by the Gileadean code as his Handmaid, is fully aware that the society in which they live warps any chance of them developing a normal reciprocal relationship. The central paradox is that while clearly a rather pleasant and gentle individual on a personal level, in a wider context the Commander not only benefits from and enforces the laws of the theocracy but in fact helped to design and codify them, according to the research of Professor Pieixoto as recounted in the Historical Notes at the end of the novel.

Section IX Night: Chapter 24

Chapter 24: Offred analyses her relationship with the Commander

Back in her own room, Offred decides that she may be able to manipulate the Commander, using sex as a weapon. She remembers a film about the Nazi Holocaust in which a concentration camp guard's mistress sought to defend him as a decent human being, and considers the problem of separating any one individual from the corrupt and twisted regime that they embody. Her nerves strung out like piano wire, Offred struggles to suppress a bout of hysterical laughter and falls asleep with her head inside the closet that bears the enigmatic inscription.

Commentary This chapter draws an explicit link between the Commander and those who readily carried out Hitler's orders. Offred struggles to separate the man from the regime that he not only helped to establish but enthusiastically serves.

Section X Soul Scrolls: Chapters 25–29

Chapter 25: Offred and the Commander play Scrabble

The secret meetings between Offred and the Commander continue behind Serena Joy's back. At night in his study they play Scrabble, she reads fashion magazines and he gives her some forbidden hand lotion.

Commentary Scrabble is a game in which players score points by using small letter tiles to form whole words, as if completing a crossword with no clues. This innocent and old-fashioned family board game takes on a whole new meaning within the Republic of Gilead; when women are forbidden to read, the innocuous pleasures it affords acquire the heady aura of forbidden sex. As Offred notes in Chapter 24 with ironic amusement, '**Context is all**'.

Top ten quotation

Chapter 26: The Commander and Offred grow closer

Offred's complex relationship with the Commander is beginning to affect not only her feelings for him but also for Serena Joy. Although she has never had sex with the Commander outside the confines of the Ceremony, the growing emotional bond between them means that she is now essentially his mistress. The Commander almost gives himself away by touching Offred's face as they have sex during another Ceremony; this gesture would be enough to get her labelled an Unwoman were the jealous Serena Joy to see.

Commentary As Offred's relationship with the Commander develops, she begins to feel differently during the Ceremony. Her growing emotional involvement means that she is no longer merely his Handmaid. The classic love triangle of husband, wife and mistress seems to be developing in precisely the sort of messy and uncontrolled way that the complex sexual rules of the theocracy were designed to prevent. Offred knows that Serena Joy, who already resents her, would actively loathe her if she discovered that the Handmaid was having sex with Commander Fred beyond the rigid confines of the Ceremony. Given this context, Offred thinks back to her time at the Red Centre, when Aunt Lydia said that in time, Handmaids would be like daughters to the Commanders' Wives. The chances of this cosy theory ever being put into practice seem vanishingly small; it is impossible to imagine such an essentially warped and unequal relationship ever being normalised.

Chapter 27: Offred and Ofglen visit the prayer shop

Ofglen and Offred visit Soul Scrolls, a shop where the Wives phone in orders for printed prayers as a way of publicly advertising their spirituality. When Ofglen tests Offred by asking if she thinks God ever listens to these prayers, Offred

Context

In listing the endless series of unjust punishments and miseries inflicted on women during the establishment of the Gileadean regime, Atwood can be seen as recasting the Old Testament story of Job. Job is a righteous man whose faith God allows the Devil to test; despite the Devil's best efforts, the faithful Job refuses to curse God. The Book of Job is the Bible's most famous example of the age-old problem of the suffering of the innocent.

finds the courage to say no. At this, Ofglen tells Offred that she works for an underground resistance movement that aims to overthrow the theocracy. When one of the black vans used by the secret police stops, the terrified Offred thinks she is about to be arrested – but the Eyes trap someone else.

Commentary The fact that Offred is prepared to risk trusting Ofglen shows the extent to which she is changing. When she tells her fellow Handmaid that she has no faith in the Wives' prayers, she is calling into question the entire theocratic power structure of the Republic and, had Ofglen been an informer, this remark would have been more than enough to condemn Offred to exile in the Colonies.

Chapter 28: Offred remembers: the Gileadean coup

Offred remembers the coup that toppled the government of the USA and how Moira first alerted her to the full implications of what was happening. With frightening speed women were denied access to their own bank accounts and fired from their jobs and, while Luke was distressed at the turn of events, the new imbalance of power between the couple began to drive a wedge between them. Offred compares her failure to protest against the coup with the active feminism of her mother's generation.

Commentary The society Offred describes is one in which pornography and prostitution are parts of everyday life. As the ubiquitous 'Pornomarts' led to conservative-inspired 'porn riots', through a fatal combination of lethargy and complacency, it seems, the rights gained for women by the early feminist campaigners were forfeited.

Chapter 29: The Commander confides in Offred

The Commander tells Offred that the mysterious Latin phrase in her bedroom cupboard means 'Don't let the bastards grind you down', and that the Handmaid who wrote it hanged herself. Realising she might be able to take advantage of his growing feelings for her, Offred asks the Commander to tell her what's going on.

Commentary This chapter reveals not only the dysfunctionality of the Commander's marriage but also the terrible danger inherent in arousing the jealousy of Serena Joy. Speaking of the suicide of the previous Handmaid, Commander Fred's words are chilling. '"Serena found out," he says, as if this explains it. And it does' (Atwood 1996: 197). Despite his apparent boyish friendliness, given what he knows of his wife's capacity for exacting a deadly revenge on any woman she sees as having betrayed her, the reader must wonder at his willingness to put Offred at risk in exactly the same way. Significantly, when he expresses his pity for a woman's suffering, it is not for the Handmaid he coerced into a secret relationship that led directly to her death, but for Cora, the unfortunate Martha who discovered her corpse.

Section XI Night: Chapter 30

Chapter 30: Offred remembers: planning the escape; Offred's prayer

Conscious of her growing feelings for Nick, Offred thinks back to her failed escape attempt and realises with horror that anyone could have betrayed her and Luke. She prays as she has never prayed before, but finds no comfort. The chapter ends with her contemplating suicide.

Commentary Offred remembers that Luke had to dispose of their pet cat before they made their escape attempt, in case her mewing and scratching around the empty house alerted the neighbours to the family's disappearance. The death of this innocent animal foreshadows the numerous victims of the regime. Her memories of Luke and her child are fading like a burning photograph; in a memorably tragic image, the 'blackness eats them'. In her loneliness and despair, Offred recites her own version of the Pater Noster or Lord's Prayer; the childlike simplicity of the original, as taught by Jesus to his disciples, no longer seems applicable to the paradoxically unchristian situation in which she finds herself.

Taking it further ▶

The title of Carol Ann Duffy's 2002 poetry collection *Feminine Gospels* reflects the poet's wish to rewrite the 'gospel truth' of scripture from a female point of view. In 'The Virgin's Memo', which features in this collection, the Mother of God drops some gentle hints to her son about how the world might have been a little better organised. Compare Offred's prayer with this poem and think about the ways in which each text presents some of the issues that feminists perceive in the marginalised position of women within organised religion.

> ### Context
>
> Remind yourself of the words of the original Pater Noster, which forms part of Jesus' Sermon on the Mount in the Gospel of Matthew (6:9-13). The structure of the original prayer consists of three statements to God followed by four entreaties related to our everyday needs and wishes. How far does Offred's prayer (pp.204-5) follow and diverge from that of Jesus?

Section XII Jezebel's: Chapters 31–39

Chapter 31: Ofglen and Serena Joy offer secret alliances

Ofglen tells Offred that the password of the Gileadean resistance is 'Mayday' and warns her of the dangers of being captured and betraying her comrades. Serena Joy tells Offred that the fact that she is still not pregnant indicates that the Commander may be infertile, and that she will have a better chance of avoiding being exiled as an Unwoman if she sleeps with Nick instead. She offers to let Offred see a picture of her lost daughter if she goes along with the deception.

Commentary 'Mayday', the resistance movement's code word, comes from the French phrase 'm'aidez' meaning 'help me'. An international signal indicating that the speaker is in urgent distress, the Mayday call is associated with situations of extreme danger. Its adoption by the Gileadean underground thus conveys their passionate opposition to the rule of the theocracy. In her own way, Serena Joy is being equally subversive; in hinting that the Commander is sterile she is exposing one of the Republic's greatest sexist myths. She is effectively acting as a fifth columnist – a secret agent who, in seeking to undermine a system or society from within, can be the most dangerous kind of revolutionary of all. When his Wife and Handmaid plot to deceive the Commander together, it seems that the brutality of the theocracy has backfired for once in serving to unite rather than divide the women in his life. It is significant that while both Ofglen and Serena Joy provide evidence of Gileadean women forming subversive secret pacts to undermine the dictates of the regime, Atwood deftly juxtaposes in this chapter the selfless bravery of the former with the selfish treachery of the latter.

Chapter 32: Offred's feelings for the Commander and his former Handmaid

Offred describes her clandestine visits to Commander Fred's study. He seems to enjoy flouting the norms and rules of Gileadean society in order to showcase his own power. He tells Offred that before the revolution, feminism had made men feel almost redundant and incapable of forming positive relationships with women. He puts forward the view that life is now much better for men and that 'you can't make an omelette without breaking eggs'. His views alienate the narrator and she begins to consider his relationship with the former Offred.

Commentary Offred is surprised at the Commander's breathtakingly selfish views on men and women, pointing out that in pre-Gileadean times American society was saturated with sex, with Pornycorners – presumably brothels or sex shops – on virtually every street. Surprisingly he argues that it was not a lack of sex that was creating problems, but a lack of power and the primal thrill of the chase: 'There was nothing to work for, nothing to fight for.' Following this chilling insight into the Commander's psyche, Offred thinks once again of her predecessor, the Handmaid who escaped only by hanging herself; once her lifeless body was swinging from the ceiling light cord she was 'safe then, protected altogether'. The narrator is beginning to feel seriously frightened.

Chapter 33: Going to the Prayvaganza; Offred hears news of Janine

Ofglen and Offred attend a Women's Prayvaganza in which the different groups – Wives, Handmaids, Marthas, Econowives, *et al.* – are strictly segregated. The two Handmaids head for the back of their cordoned-off standing-room section so they can talk more freely. Ofglen shares the gossip that Janine's baby girl, Angela, was actually a deformed Unbaby and that Janine had in fact slept with her doctor in order to get pregnant. Offred remembers an incident at the Red Centre when Janine behaved in such a strange and distant manner that it seemed akin to some kind of nervous breakdown; significantly it was Moira who managed to snap Janine out of her trance before she was discovered by the Aunts.

Commentary Janine's story is a fearful warning of the psychological and emotional toll exacted of the Handmaids as mere **'two-legged wombs'**. Little Angela is firstly described as 'Janine's baby' before the narrator correctly redefines her as 'the baby that passed through Janine on its way to somewhere else.' Offred recognises the vulnerable Janine's propensity to blame herself and recalls a chilling episode in which she regressed to her past life as a waitress when being brainwashed by the Aunts at the Red Centre. Once again Moira and Janine are directly juxtaposed to allow the reader to compare their oppositional fight-and-flight reactions to their indoctrination by the Gileadean regime.

> Top ten quotation

CRITICAL VIEW

Janine/Ofwarren's distressing psychological symptoms seem to suggest that she suffered an episode of dissociative fugue during her time at the Red Centre. A fugue state is a rare psychiatric condition in which the patient undergoes a severe identity crisis, often sparked by a period of intense physical or emotional stress. At times people may even seek to establish a new identity while in a fugue state, only to then undergo an episode of amnesia. Examine Atwood's presentation of Janine/Ofwarren in the light of this psychological reading.

Chapter 34: The Prayvaganza

In this chapter the reader learns that Prayvaganzas are mass single-sex religious celebrations. The gender divide here is absolute, as Prayvaganzas tend to be group weddings for women and military jamborees for men, 'the things we are supposed to rejoice in the most, respectively,' the narrator points out (Atwood 1996: 232). Offred goes on to recall both the Commander's assertion that women are looked after and protected within the context of an arranged marriage, and Aunt Lydia's claim that Gileadean women should live harmoniously together. Ofglen asks Offred to spy on the Commander for the benefit of the underground resistance.

Commentary In blending the words 'prayer' and 'extravaganza', Atwood stresses an essential paradox; whereas Jesus taught the importance of praying silently and alone, in a theocratic state the act has become one of hysterical and ostentatious public display. This showbiz-style event is linked with the Wives' hollow and self-aggrandising purchases of prayers from Soul Scrolls; in Gilead, religion has become associated with outward show as opposed to private piety. Atwood's mordant wit shines through at times here; when the Commander in charge intones that women should 'continue in faith and charity and holiness with sobriety,' the feisty Ofglen undercuts him: '"He should tell that to the

▶ The Prayvaganza, from the 1990 film

Context

The concept of the cult mass wedding ceremony is closely associated with the notorious Unification Church founded by Sun Myung Moon (1920–2012), among others. Moon, a controversial figure whose followers were popularly (and unsurprisingly) known as Moonies, was jailed for tax fraud in the USA before anointing himself the 'Messiah' in 2004.

Wives," Ofglen murmurs, "when they're into the sherry."' (Atwood 1996: 233). Yet this humour is juxtaposed with the chilling description of the Prayvaganzas occasionally held for nuns who have 'recanted'.

There is a special hatred and fear of nuns in Gilead, because by refusing to participate in the sexual rites demanded of fertile young women and by declaring themselves married to God, they pose an overt threat to the iron control the republican authorities insist on exerting over women's bodies. Their refusal to have sex at all is interpreted as a greater challenge to the Gileadean order than that posed by the prostitutes who work at the brothel, Jezebel's. In maintaining their right not to have sex, the nuns are seen as undermining the theocracy's goal of repopulating the country. In the topsy-turvy world of Gilead, a nun who insists on her right not to submit to what is in effect legalised rape will be labelled an Unwoman and banished to the Colonies; the hideous irony is hard to overstate. In a tragic parody of the ways in which postulant (trainee) nuns exchange a white veil for a black one when they make their permanent vows of poverty, chastity and obedience to God, Atwood presents the arresting visual image of the nuns being forced to 'take the red veil' of the Handmaid during the special Prayvaganzas (Atwood 1996: 232). Characterised as 'mysterious and exotic' witches, Offred notes the lengths that the regime has to go to in order to break the nuns down as they spend time in 'Solitary' (Atwood 1996: 232). 'None of us likes to draw one for a shopping partner,' admits Offred. 'They are more broken than the rest of us; it's hard to feel comfortable with them' (Atwood 1996: 233).

Chapter 35: Offred remembers the escape; Serena Joy shows Offred a photograph of her daughter

Offred remembers trying to flee across the border into Canada with Luke and weeps at the memory of her lost love. When Serena Joy shows Offred a photograph of her daughter, the pain she experiences is almost unbearable.

Commentary Offred's nostalgic private memories of falling in love come directly after the description of the glitzy public Prayvaganza; this is yet another of those powerfully ironic juxtapositions which Atwood uses to draw attention to her main themes and ideas. Here we see that whatever those glossy choreographed Prayvaganzas are celebrating, it surely isn't 'love' as we understand it – messy, complex and infuriating as that may be. The chapter ends with a heartbreakingly poignant description of Offred's response to being shown a photograph of her daughter that has come into Serena Joy's possession via a 'network of the Marthas' (Atwood 1996: 240). In reversing the common image of a fading photograph by having Offred see *herself* as fading, Atwood vividly dramatises how the narrator's belief in herself as a mother is being suppressed and denied:

> Time has not stood still. It has washed over me, washed me away, as if I'm nothing more than a woman of sand, left by a careless child too near the water. I have been obliterated for her. I am only a shadow now, far back behind the glib shiny surface of this photograph. A shadow of a shadow, as dead mothers become. You can see it in her eyes: I am not there.

> But she exists, in her white dress. She grows and lives. Isn't that a good thing? A blessing?

> Still, I can't bear it, to have been erased like that. Better she'd brought me nothing.

> (Atwood 1996: 240)

Chapter 36: Offred dresses up for a night out with the Commander

The Commander asks Offred to wear a sexy burlesque-style pre-Gileadean costume and make-up underneath one of Serena Joy's blue robes. Nick drives them to Jezebel's, a secret brothel; if asked, she is to say she is an 'evening rental', or prostitute.

Commentary The iconography of the clothes the Commander chooses for Offred is striking. In Victorian times it was hard for women to avoid being categorised as one of two polarised stereotypes: the pure and virtuous domestic 'angel in the house' or the sexually voracious 'fallen' woman. These binary opposites were symbolised by Jesus' mother, the Madonna, and the prostitute Mary Magdalene. These extreme ideas about women seem to have been revived and given new force within the Gileadean regime, which has gone beyond anything envisaged by the Victorians to impose a dress code that externalises the roles available to women. In dressing Offred as a striptease artist, only to make her conceal this sexual identity with his Wife's Madonna-blue robe, the Commander illustrates the ways in which the inflexible stringency of the virgin/whore opposition warps and distorts the ways in which men respond to women.

The Commander's obsessive interest in clothes and clothing would seem to support Professor Pieixoto's post-Gileadean identification of him in the Historical Notes as the real-life 'Frederick R. Waterford', who was 'responsible for the design of the female costumes and for the suggestion that the Handmaids wear red, which he seems to have borrowed from the uniforms of German prisoners of war in Canadian "P.O.W." camps of the Second World War era' (Atwood 1996: 319).

Chapter 37: The Commander takes Offred to Jezebel's

Jezebel's occupies an old hotel where Offred once met Luke. The Commander admits that while the brothel is illegal, men can never be satisfied sexually by just one woman. Offred sees Moira and they silently signal their intention to meet in the toilets.

Commentary According to Commander Fred, men need to sleep around because it is in the interests of the human race: '**Nature demands variety for men. It's part of the procreational strategy. It's Nature's plan**' (Atwood 1996: 249). This classic piece of hypocritical self-justification reminds us that for all his superficial pleasantness, he is part of a patriarchal culture that is predicated upon sexual inequality and injustice. In allowing Offred to wear something other than her Handmaid's robe and taking her away from her dreary imprisonment for even a single night, it may seem that he is offering her a taste of the liberty that has long been denied her. In fact, of course, in effectively dressing her up as a sex worker and taking her to a brothel, the Commander is only debasing and oppressing her in another — arguably even more creepily sinister — manner.

Top ten quotation

CRITICAL VIEW

Think about the implications of the femme fatale figure, as represented here by Queen Jezebel, from a feminist standpoint. What do you make of the idea that men are not always responsible for their actions, but can be led astray by evil women?

Context

The fact that the brothel is named Jezebel's is deeply ironic. In the Old Testament, Queen Jezebel was a godless femme fatale whose manipulation of her weak husband, Ahab, brought disaster on Israel. Her fate was to be thrown out of a window before having her dead body eaten by stray dogs.

In another of the arrestingly powerful and detailed descriptions of women that pepper the novel, the reader meets the gallant Moira once more, this time dressed as a Playboy Bunny. Worn by the waitresses at Hugh Hefner's Playboy Clubs, 'bunny suits' were shiny, strapless, corset-like outfits complemented by a collar and cuffs that mocked the tuxedo jackets often worn by the male customers. This culturally iconic ensemble was topped off with fake bunny ears and a fluffy tail:

She's dressed absurdly, in a black outfit of once-shiny satin that looks the worse for wear. It's strapless, wired from the inside, pushing up the breasts, but it doesn't quite fit Moira, it's too large, so that one breast is plumped out and the other one isn't. She's tugging absent-mindedly at the top, pulling it up. There's a wad of cotton attached to the back, I can see it as she half-turns; it looks like a sanitary pad that's been popped like a piece of popcorn. I realise that it's supposed to be a tail. Attached to her head are two ears, of a rabbit or deer, it's not easy to tell; one of the ears has lost its starch or wiring and is flopping halfway down. She has a black bow tie around her neck and is wearing black net stockings and black high heels. She always hated high heels.

(Atwood 1996: 251)

▲ A classic 1960s Playboy Bunny in stereotypical costume

Context

The idea of the lesbian feminist Moira dressing up as a Playboy Bunny is both blackly comic and hugely ironic. Over half a century ago, feminist writer Gloria Steinem famously revealed the exploitation and sexualised abuse suffered by many of these young women in 'A Bunny's Tale', which she wrote after working undercover at a Playboy Club. You can read more about Steinem's ground-breaking journalistic exposé in the *Guardian* online (a full web address can be found on p.103).

Chapter 38: Moira's story

Moira tells Offred what happened after her escape from the Red Centre. She nearly made it to freedom using the Underground Femaleroad but was caught and tortured by the secret police. Forced to watch films about the dreaded Colonies – where the Gileadean regime sends its undesirables to undertake unspeakable work cleaning up radioactive spills and where life expectancy is barely three years – Moira has finally submitted to the regime and has opted to work at Jezebel's rather than go into exile. After this chance meeting, Offred never sees Moira again.

Commentary Moira's story is an embedded narrative – that is, a story within a story. It functions as a kind of elegy or requiem as Offred laments the loss of her dear friend and mentor. Moira's tale of exciting hairsbreadth escapes, nail-biting tension, extreme danger and exceptional bravery seems to belong to a different type of text – an adventure yarn or action thriller. The details of the Underground Femaleroad offer a clear parallel with the Underground Railroad that moved escaped slaves in the American South from safe house to safe house and on to freedom in the North before and during the Civil War (1861–65).

On one level, of course, Moira's fate is horrific and tragic. It is difficult to accept that this brave and funny woman is now dressed in a bedraggled and ill-fitting Playboy Bunny costume and living on borrowed time. But, crucially, the doomed Moira has *chosen* to become a Jezebel rather than be exiled as an Unwoman.

With her trademark sparky wit, she teases Offred by claiming that in having reached the end of the road, paradoxically she has found a kind of last-minute freedom. Sexually, for example, Moira says she is now in 'Butch paradise', since many of the formerly heterosexual Jezebels have turned to lesbianism: 'The Aunts figure we're all damned anyway,' she wisecracks, 'they've given up on us, so it doesn't matter what sort of vice we get up to, and the Commanders don't give a piss what we do in our off-time. Anyway, women on women sort of turns them on' (Atwood 1996: 262). Deftly, as she has so often before, Moira puts her finger on the rank hypocrisy of the Gileadean high command, as they privately allow (and are even thrilled by) what they would publicly condemn as outright apostasy. This crucial chapter ends with a metafictional flourish, as Offred riffs once again on the impossibility of telling the right story. Note how she seems to refer to *Moira herself* as an unfinished narrative here – a tale whose ending is both unknown and unknowable:

> Here is what I'd like to tell. I'd like to tell a story about how Moira escaped, for good this time. Or if I couldn't tell that, I'd like to say she blew up Jezebel's, with fifty Commanders inside it. I'd like her to end with something daring and spectacular, some outrage, something that would befit her. But, as far as I know that didn't happen. I don't know how she ended, or even if she did, because I never saw her again.
>
> (Atwood 1996: 262)

Context

During her escape attempt, Moira is helped by some Quakers. Quakers (officially known as members of the Religious Society of Friends) practise a form of Christianity notable for its enlightened treatment of women and avoidance of hierarchical power structures. In Quaker worship, rather than listening to a sermon preached by a minister, anyone who feels called to speak may do so; the emphasis is on the individual's personal experience of God. Historically, Quakers were prominent campaigners for social justice, e.g. for the abolition of the slave trade and for prison reform.

Building critical skills

In order to extend your understanding of Margaret Atwood's attitude to organised religion, list as many reasons as you can why the Quakers would be fundamentally opposed to the form of Christianity practised by the Republic of Gilead.

Chapter 39: Offred and the Commander

When the Commander takes Offred to a hotel room for sex, it is an eerie reminder of the time when she was Luke's mistress. Unlike the Commander, she feels no pleasure at the thought of their sexual encounter and knows that she will have to pretend to enjoy it.

Commentary This chapter both evokes and distorts the reader's memory of the Ceremony. Offred cannot fake enjoyment while they have sex this time, despite the Commander's attempts to make it seem like a traditional 'date'. The Commander is sorry that he cannot have his cake and eat it – i.e. enjoy both an arranged marriage to Serena Joy and a passionate romance with a mistress; he completely fails to realise that forced sex can never generate the spontaneous feelings he longs for. Their sexual encounter is not the private relationship he craves but a highly politicised power trip; shockingly, Offred feels that the Ceremony at least has a basic honesty about it that this encounter lacks.

CRITICAL VIEW

Some radical feminists feel that it is impossible for any heterosexual relationship to be equal and non-hierarchical if it takes place within an oppressive patriarchal society. They argue that women who have sexual relationships with men are literally 'sleeping with the enemy'. What is your response to Offred's relationship with the Commander in the light of this view? How might one view Moira's lesbianism through this critical lens?

Section XIII Night: Chapter 40

Chapter 40: Offred and Nick

Serena Joy tells Offred to go to Nick's apartment and the reader gets different versions of their lovemaking, any or all of which might be 'true'. Offred cannot avoid thinking about Luke after making love to Nick.

Commentary This chapter again showcases one of Atwood's signature structural techniques, in juxtaposing Offred's diametrically opposed sexual encounters with the Commander and Nick, both of which occur on the same night. Unlike her earlier time with Commander Fred, which was both oppressive and faintly ridiculous, Offred makes love to Nick as a way of nostalgically rekindling something of the old-fashioned romance that lovers enjoyed in pre-Gileadean days. Moreover, this chapter is notably metafictional in that Offred hazards three versions of their narrative of love before admitting that none of them is true. '**I made that up**,' she says at one point. '**It didn't happen that way. Here is what happened**'; later, having offered an alternative account, she admits, 'It didn't happen that way either. I'm not sure how it happened; not exactly.' Yet paradoxically the narrator is conscious that her very unreliability testifies to the impossibility of capturing in words what love really feels like: 'All I can hope for is a reconstruction: the way love feels is always only approximate' (Atwood 1996: 273; 275).

Section XIV Salvaging: Chapters 41–45

Chapter 41: Offred discusses storytelling and describes her relationship with Nick

As Offred discusses the importance of telling her story, there is a sense that her narrative is hastening towards its denouement. Her illicit night-time meetings with Nick continue behind the backs of both the Commander and Serena Joy, and they begin to develop an honest and intimate relationship. Meanwhile, Ofglen urges her to spy on the Commander.

Taking it further ▶

Margaret Atwood has explained that the political aspects of her research for *The Handmaid's Tale* were reinforced by conversations with many people who had lived through persecution under evil regimes, including 'a woman who had been in the French Resistance during the [Second World] war' (Atwood 2005: 96). Research the women who worked to liberate France during the German occupation, then consider how Ofglen and Moira can be seen as following in their footsteps.

◁ Top ten quotation

Commentary Once again Offred discusses the art of storytelling, beginning this chapter by expressing her dissatisfaction with how things are going, narratively speaking:

> I wish this story were different. I wish it were more civilised. I wish it showed me in a better light, if not happier, then at least more active, less hesitant, less distracted by trivia. I wish it had more shape. I wish it were about love, or about sudden realisations important to one's life, or even about sunsets, birds, rainstorms, or snow.
>
> (Atwood 1996: 279)

Yet despite its limitations and inadequacies, storytelling is put forward as an act of resistance. Offred knows she is no Moira or Ofglen, but then she is no Janine either; moreover, in bearing witness she plays her own small part in undermining the theocracy. 'By telling you anything at all, I'm at least believing in you, I believe you're there, I believe you into being. Because I'm telling you this story I will your existence. I tell, therefore you are' (Atwood 1996: 279). This throwaway pun, based on the French philosopher René Descartes' famous dictum 'I think, therefore I am', shows that Offred has not lost her sense of humour even with the walls seemingly closing in on her. Descartes' original Latin phrase *Cogito, ergo sum* suggests that in *thinking* about one's own existence, one *proves* one's own existence; in Gilead, Offred's thoughts, feelings, dreams and stories similarly attest to *her* existence, in and of themselves, regardless of what they are actually 'about'. Notice how Offred deliberately contrasts the ways she feels when having sex with the Commander and when making love with Nick; again Atwood juxtaposes the two men in the narrator's life in such a way as to enrich and complicate her representation of men in the text as a whole.

Building critical skills

Compare the ways in which Offred describes her feelings for Luke, Nick and Commander Fred in the novel. From a feminist perspective, do you feel that Atwood is to be criticised for paying limited attention to the suffering of men in *The Handmaid's Tale*?

Chapter 42: The Salvaging

When Offred and Ofglen attend a compulsory Salvaging (public execution) within the confines of what used to be Harvard University, it is Aunt Lydia from the Red Centre who runs the show.

Commentary The Salvaging (public hanging) of three women – including a Handmaid known as Ofcharles – takes place in the grounds of Harvard University, a location that once symbolised knowledge and freedom. The unfortunates who face execution are, horribly, 'seated on folding chairs, like graduating students who are about to be given prizes' (Atwood 1996: 285). As Offred knows only too well, '**Context is all**'; now that the building lies at the very heart of the Gileadean Republic, it symbolises ignorance and slavery. It is as horrifying as if Cambridge University in the UK were to be turned into a government detention centre where people would be routinely tortured to death.

Top ten quotation

The evil at the heart of the theocracy is revealed once again when the Handmaids – who are placed right at the front of the crowd 'where everyone can keep an eye on us' (Atwood 1996: 285) – are forced to make a public sign of accepting that Ofcharles has committed a crime worthy of capital punishment, even though, for the first time, no details of what she is supposed to have done have been announced. As Offred declares, '[I've] placed my hand on my heart to show my unity with the Salvagers and my consent, and my complicity in the death of this woman' (Atwood 1996: 288). In terms of structure, it is notable that Atwood entwines the private story of Offred's love for Nick with a series of vividly described and appallingly violent public deaths. What chance do these young lovers have of finding happiness, the reader wonders, when they live within such a society?

Chapter 43: The Particicution

The Salvaging is followed by a Particicution, or public lynching, in which a Guardian accused of having raped a pregnant Handmaid is torn to pieces by the Handmaids on Aunt Lydia's orders. Ofglen is the first to attack, but she later tells Offred that the man was a member of Mayday and that she had acted to spare him further agony.

Commentary This chapter begins with an arresting description of the three women hanged during the Salvaging; they are likened to dead birds, 'chickens strung up by their necks in a meatshop window; like birds with their wings clipped, like flightless birds, wrecked angels' (Atwood 1996: 289). The reader may be reminded of how Offred saw herself when dressed up in her tatty pink feather dress for her visit to Jezebel's. We can see this as another example of Atwood's holding together the disparate sections of a fragmented and challenging text by incorporating repeating tropes and patterns.

Following the Salvaging, Aunt Lydia announces with all the pizazz of a fairground barker that a second public horror show is to unfold. The reader may think nothing could be worse than the Salvaging, but the next stage in the proceedings requires the Handmaids to do much more than passively acquiesce; a Particicution is, as its name suggests, an execution in which they must all participate. '"You know the rules for a Particicution," Aunt Lydia says. "You will wait until I blow the whistle. After that, what you do is up to you, until I blow the whistle again. Understood?"' (Atwood 1996: 290). The behaviour of Ofglen initially seems utterly out of character and appals Offred: 'She pushes him down, sideways, then kicks his head viciously, one, two, three times, sharp painful jabs with the foot, well-aimed' (Atwood 1996: 291). Yet all becomes clear when Ofglen reveals the truth about the victim: 'He wasn't a rapist at all, he was a political. He was one of ours. I knocked him out. Put him out of his misery. Don't you know what they're doing to him?' (Atwood 1996: 292).

> **Building critical skills**
>
> The symbolic transmutation of Harvard University – whose Latin motto is 'Veritas', meaning 'truth' – into a venue for public torture recalls the oxymoronic mottos enforced by the Party in George Orwell's *Nineteen Eighty-Four*: *'WAR IS PEACE, FREEDOM IS SLAVERY, IGNORANCE IS STRENGTH'*. To what extent can the Gileadean Republic's treatment of women be considered in line with the last two of these mottos?

▲ The Particicution, from the 1990 film

Communal violence is a frightening social phenomenon that can occur when a strong feeling of solidarity among members of a particular ethnic or religious group allows and encourages them to attack others whom they perceive to be 'different'. In Gilead, singling out and scapegoating 'sinners' reinforces the sense of community among the 'righteous'. The climax of the scene is the appearance of Ofwarren/Janine towards the end. Her behaviour during this shocking event shows that the formerly submissive Handmaid has now tipped over into outright madness as a result of living under the Gileadean regime. The fact that throughout the text both of her names have been used interchangeably is significant; the double label symbolises her extremely fragile and increasingly fragmented sense of self. Within this scene, however, which is the last mention of this character in the text, Offred calls her – and indeed addresses her directly as – 'Janine'. The description of her appearance and manner following the Particicution is stark in its horrific simplicity:

> There's a smear of blood across her cheek, and more of it on the white of her headdress. She's smiling, a bright diminutive smile. Her eyes have come loose.
>
> 'Hi there,' she says. 'How are you doing?' She's holding something, tightly, in her right hand. It's a clump of blond hair. She gives a small giggle.
>
> 'Janine,' I say. But she's let go, totally now, she's in free fall, she's in withdrawal.
>
> 'You have a nice day,' she says, and walks on past us, towards the gate.
>
> (Atwood 1996: 292)

For Janine, who was gang-raped as a teenager (for which Aunt Lydia makes her admit she was to blame), the opportunity to attack a 'rapist' seems to offer a twisted kind of justice. It is clear that she has finally regressed to her former life, as she mechanically repeats the standard phrases she used to greet her customers with when she worked as a waitress. Structurally, of course, this incident should remind the reader of the time when Janine previously exhibited distressing signs of severe mental illness during her incarceration at the Red Centre, which was described in Chapter 33; she reiterated her comforting waitress' mantras then, too. 'Hello, she said, but not to me,' Offred remembers. 'My name's Janine. I'm your waitperson for this morning. Can I get you some coffee to begin with?' (Atwood 1996: 228). On that occasion Moira had explicitly told Offred how to deal with any future evidence of mental disturbance from Janine; '"She does that again and I'm not here," Moira said to me, "you just have to slap her like that. You can't let her go slipping over the edge. That stuff is catching"' (Atwood 1996: 229). But now that Janine *is* 'doing it again', Offred is helpless to stop it. No matter that Janine did everything according to Aunt Lydia's rules; whether compliant or rebellious, the 'bastards' of the Gileadean regime can and will, it seems, grind everyone down in the end.

Chapter 44: Ofglen disappears

One day when Offred goes shopping, she is met by a total stranger who announces that *she* is Ofglen. When Offred tries to assess whether the new Ofglen is also part of the underground resistance by referring guardedly to 'May Day', it seems clear that she is not. Moreover, she delivers the terrifying news that the former Ofglen hanged herself rather than face arrest.

Commentary From this point on, the narrative begins to move more quickly as Atwood ratchets up the narrative tension by creating an ominous sense of time running out for Offred. It is clear that the new Ofglen recognises the 'May Day' code word, but her response is chilling: '"That isn't a term I remember. I'm surprised you do. You ought to make an effort…" She pauses. "To clear your mind of such…" She pauses again. "Echoes"' (Atwood 1996: 296). The sinister replacement of Ofglen is a reminder that in Gilead, Handmaids are merely interchangeable commodities; after all, the narrator herself is merely a relabelled substitute for Commander Fred's former concubine. Now that two of the three narratively important Handmaids the reader has met during the course of the novel have met terrible ends, with Ofwarren driven to madness and Ofglen to suicide, Atwood encourages the reader to wonder what terrible fate is in store for Offred, the only survivor.

Chapter 45: Serena Joy accuses Offred

Despite her respect and liking for Ofglen, the other Handmaid's death at least eases Offred's terror that Ofglen might under torture have reported her to the secret police. The narrator is now utterly terrified and feels there is nothing she will not do to go on living. But it is too late. When she gets back to the house,

Building critical skills

Offred guardedly mentions "the first of May … What they used to call May Day" to see if the new Ofglen recognises the code word of the underground resistance (Atwood 1996: 296). As well as being a traditional spring holiday, in the late nineteenth century 1 May was adopted as International Workers' Day by left-wing groups. What might be Atwood's possible reasons for adding a politicised meaning to this in terms of rebellion and resistance to an oppressive regime?

Serena Joy is waiting for her, armed with the evidence of the Handmaid's betrayal in the shape of her own winter robe, now stained with lipstick from Offred's visit to Jezebel's.

Commentary With this very short chapter consisting of just two pages, we have almost reached the end of Offred's story. The way in which she reports her feelings on the death of Ofglen clearly references the ultimate sacrifice of Christ on the cross: 'So she's dead, and I am safe after all. She did it before they came. I feel great relief. I feel thankful to her. She has died that I may live' (Atwood 1996: 298). Ofglen's fate has not inspired Offred to wish to follow in her footsteps; quite the contrary.

With Moira gone, Janine insane and Ofglen dead, the narrator is the last woman standing and is understandably desperate to keep it that way. She swears to God that she will do anything He requires: 'I'll sacrifice. I'll repent. I'll abdicate. I'll renounce' (Atwood 1996: 298). Interestingly, when Serena Joy furiously accuses Offred of following in the footsteps of their previous Handmaid by wearing her own Madonna blue robe to cover up the sexy costume chosen by Commander Fred, Atwood suggests that Serena Joy too is deserving of some pity. As she brandishes the shoddy costume that Offred wore underneath her cloak, the reader sees her vulnerability as the clothing seems to pulse with a poisonous evil of its own. 'The purple sequins fall, slithering down over the step like snakeskin, glittering in the sunlight. "Behind my back," she says. "You could have left me something." Does she love him after all? She raises her cane. I think she is going to hit me, but she doesn't. "Pick up that disgusting thing and get to your room. Just like the other one. A slut. You'll end up the same."' (Atwood 1996: 299). Offred's fate seems clear and the reader at last knows for sure why her predecessor killed herself. Sleeping with Commander Fred may be an effective death sentence if his jealous and vengeful Wife finds out.

Section XV Night: Chapter 46

Chapter 46: Offred is taken away

Offred waits as the secret police arrive; she assumes they have come to arrest her following a tip-off from the vindictive Serena Joy. Nick tells her that the van's occupants are in fact members of Mayday. As she passes the Commander and his Wife in the hallway, it seems clear that he, too, is a marked man. The Handmaid leaves the house for the last time, her fate seemingly uncertain.

Commentary In her room Offred reviews her possible courses of action: setting fire to the bed, escaping out of the window via a rope of knotted bedsheets, begging the Commander for mercy, attacking Serena Joy. In the end, of course, it is the ghost of the room's former occupant who shows her the way:

> Behind me I feel her presence, my ancestress, my double, turning in mid-air under the chandelier, in her costume of stars and feathers, a bird stopped in flight, a woman made into an angel, waiting to be

Context

The figure of the double or doppelgänger – essentially a second self – has often been used to explore the duality of human nature. One classic example of this is Robert Louis Stevenson's Gothic novella *The Strange Case of Dr Jekyll and Mr Hyde* (1886).

found. By me this time. How could I have believed I was alone in here? There were always two of us. Get it over, she says. I'm tired of all this melodrama, I'm tired of keeping silent. There's no one you can protect, your life has value to no one. I want it finished.

(Atwood 1996: 305)

Before Offred can commit suicide, however, Nick comes to her room to fetch her. But things are not quite as they seem. The narrator herself does not know if Nick can be trusted when he tells her that the Eyes who have come to arrest her are in fact members of Mayday. One glimmer of hope may be seen in that he calls her by her real name. Offred's story seems to end on a cliffhanger, with the narrator apparently poised between the '**darkness**' of recapture and the '**light**' of escape. In a 1986 *New York Times* interview, just a year after the novel was published, however, Margaret Atwood made it plain which of these two endings is in fact the true one. Stating that the book 'isn't totally bleak and pessimistic', she tells us that:

> [the] central character – the Handmaid Offred – gets out. The possibility of escape exists. A society exists in the future which is not the society of Gilead and is capable of reflecting about the society of Gilead in the same way that we reflect about the seventeenth century. Her little message in a bottle has gotten through to someone – which is about all we can hope, isn't it?

(Atwood, in Rothstein 1986)

Moreover, in our anxiety for Offred, we mustn't overlook the fact that the omens look desperate for the Commander and Serena Joy too, both personally and politically. When he asks if the Eyes have a warrant to enter his house, the Commander is treated with scant politeness or deference: 'Not that we need one, Sir, but all is in order … Violation of state secrets' (Atwood 1996: 306). In a final deadly irony, the Handmaid has seemingly turned the tables on her Commander and his Wife:

> The Commander puts his hand to his head. What have I been saying, and to whom, and which one of his enemies has found out? Possibly he will be a security risk, now. I am above him, looking down; he is shrinking. There have already been purges among them, there will be more. Serena Joy goes white.
>
> 'Bitch,' she says. 'After all he did for you.'

(Atwood 1996: 307)

> **Top ten quotation**

Building critical skills

Explore Atwood's use of the first Offred within *The Handmaid's Tale* and trace the ways in which her experience can be seen to mirror and foreshadow what happens to her successor, the novel's narrator.

TASK

Like all totalitarian regimes, Gilead undertakes periodic purges to remove 'undesirables' and sentence them to gaol, exile or death. Research the figures of Maximilien Robespierre (1758–94) and Joseph Stalin (1879–1953) for a chilling insight into how a political regime that begins with high ideals can rapidly descend into a reign of terror.

Historical Notes

Professor Pieixoto addresses the conference

At an academic conference held many years after the fall of Gilead, Offred's story is analysed and evaluated by Professor James Darcy Pieixoto. His findings suggest that the narrator managed to reach Bangor, Maine, which is where she recorded her experiences on to some old cassette tapes that were transcribed many years later by Pieixoto and a colleague. Pieixoto suggests that – as Offred herself might say – **'Context is all'**, so that judging the theocracy by the norms and values of another time and place is inappropriate. He discusses various historical reasons behind the catastrophic decline in the birthrate, and unpicks the authorities' justifications for the extreme response to the crisis by turning to the polygamous family patterns of the Old Testament. Pieixoto's analysis of the ways in which the Republic turned to the past to formulate and justify its ideological structure chimes with Margaret Atwood's own idea that 'no society ever strays completely far from its roots' (Atwood 2005: 97). There seems to be evidence to show that similarly repressive theocracies had been established elsewhere in the former USA, in Washington and New York.

The professor has not been able to discover the identity of the narrator, but seems to have had more success identifying the Commander. He believes that he was probably either 'Frederick R. Waterford' or 'B. Frederick Judd', both powerful men who played key roles in building up the infrastructure of the Gileadean regime. On balance, he favours Waterford as Offred's Commander; this seems to chime with what the reader knows of her illicit visits to his study, as Waterford was purged for harbouring 'liberal tendencies'.

Times have certainly changed; the Native American names of Professors Johnny Running Dog and Maryann Crescent Moon suggest that the heyday of the WASP (White Anglo-Saxon Protestant) patriarchy is well and truly over.

Commentary The conference explains Gilead in a way that suggests the possibilities and limitations of academic discourse. Professor Pieixoto unpicks the technicalities of the system analytically and painstakingly, but in doing so undercuts the subjective 'truth' of the Handmaid's tale. The reader receives interesting additional information that Offred knew nothing of, such as Commander Fred's probable true identity, the fact that he was himself 'purged' by the very regime he helped to establish, and the fact that Mayday was ultimately successful in undermining the theocracy.

There is much evidence of Atwood's trademark ironic humour here, as seen in the old cassette tapes over which Offred records her narrative. Her tale overwrites a very interesting set of musicians. From Elvis Presley (the iconic Rock 'n' Roll legend who became a bloated monster addicted to prescription drugs), to the 'gender-bending' 1980s soul singer Boy George, to the vanilla kitsch conductor Mantovani, to the grunge heavy metallers Twisted Sister (who might as well have named themselves after Aunt Lydia), to the indigenous musicians

Top ten quotation

of Lithuania (a state swallowed up by the USSR during the Second World War) – each cassette tape subsumed by Offred's oral narrative taps into a highly resonant range of cultural associations.

It is crucially important to note that when we learn that the professor has transcribed Offred's story from tapes found in a safe house, the novel's open ending is undercut. This information strongly suggests that Nick *was* to be trusted and *did* manage to help Offred escape, and indeed Margaret Atwood has made it plain on more than one occasion that this is in fact what happened. In acknowledging her debt to George Orwell, the godfather of dystopian fiction, Atwood has written about how the last chapter of his iconic novel *Nineteen Eighty-Four* is an essay on Newspeak – the bizarre doublethink language concocted by Big Brother. This essay is 'written in standard English, in the third person, and in the past tense, which can only mean that the regime has fallen, and that language and individuality have survived. For whoever has written the essay on Newspeak, the world of *Nineteen Eighty-Four* is over' (Atwood 2005: 290–91). She goes on to make explicit the link with her own Historical Notes:

> *At the end of* The Handmaid's Tale, *there's a section that owes much to* Nineteen Eighty-Four. *It's the account of a symposium held several hundred years in the future, at which the repressive government described in the novel is now merely a subject for academic analysis. The parallels with Orwell's essay on Newspeak should be evident.*

(Atwood 2005: 292)

Context

George Orwell's *Nineteen Eighty-Four* is the most famous dystopian science fiction text in the English language and many of its most sinister concepts have permeated our cultural consciousness since it was first published in 1949. The adjective 'Orwellian' is now routinely used to describe the menacing tactics employed by authoritarian states to repress their citizens, while two of the novel's most iconic horrors - the all-seeing surveillance of Big Brother and the personalised nightmares of Room 101 - have both lent their names to popular television programmes.

Building critical skills

Professor Pieixoto describes the 'purging' of Commander Frederick Waterford for harbouring 'liberal tendencies' and possessing banned books and pictures. Do you think the embittered and jealous Serena Joy informed upon him, having missed her chance to get her revenge on Offred? Is this a credible proposition, based on her behaviour in Chapter 46?

Target your thinking

- What are the key themes of *The Handmaid's Tale* and how does Atwood develop them as the narrative progresses? (**AO1**)
- What narrative methods does Atwood use to illustrate and explore her key themes? (**AO2**)

Women's roles and the presentation of their bodies

Like virtually all of Atwood's novels, *The Handmaid's Tale* features a central female protagonist. The vast majority of published material about the writer's life and works is framed through the critical lens of feminism, although she has refused to be officially co-opted into the cause, perhaps fearing that to politicise her writing too overtly may weaken its creative and dramatic impact. As Heidi Sletterdahl Macpherson notes, Atwood sees herself as 'not a propagandist but an observer; her work merely reflects the reality of an uneven distribution of power between men and women' (Macpherson 2010: 23).

Atwood has stressed that the Gileadean Republic's determination to keep women strictly confined to the home meant initially imagining a future society in which the clock had been well and truly turned back:

> *My problem as a writer was, given that my society has stuffed all women back into their homes, how did they go about it? How do you get women back into their homes, now that they are running about outside the home, having jobs and generally flinging themselves around? Simple. You just close your eyes and take several giant steps back, into the not-so-very-distant past – the nineteenth century, to be exact – deprive them of the right to vote, own property or hold jobs, and prohibit public prostitution in the bargain, to keep them from hanging out on street corners, and presto, there they are, back in the home.*

(Atwood 2005: 99)

Gendered identities and roles, reproductive technologies and who controls women's bodies are fundamental concepts within this text. Atwood makes key social issues problematic in order to make the reader engage with her ideas, contesting some widely-held liberal philosophical assumptions about the way the world works. Most of us would say we are instinctively against censorship or restrictions on freedom of speech – but these very freedoms can permit the publication and dissemination of violent hard-core pornography that shows women being abused, degraded, tortured and even killed. Burning this kind of misogynist material, as Offred's mother does during a feminist rally, is clearly meant as an act of female empowerment – yet burning books is the classic act of censorship enacted by oppressive regimes, from the Renaissance monk Savonarola's Florentine Bonfire of the Vanities to the Nazis of the 1930s.

Feminist campaigners like Offred's mother argued fiercely that women should feel safe on the streets; many 'Reclaim the Night' marches took place during the 1970s and '80s, when there was widespread fear of rape. In Gilead, of course, the streets have been made perfectly safe for all women – but at what price? As Aunt Lydia says, in the 'days of anarchy, it was freedom to. Now you are being given freedom from. Don't underrate it' (Atwood 1996: 34). Which would *you* choose? the reader is asked. Many feminists claim that women support each other in a kind of global sisterhood – think of the symbolism of International Women's Day every March, for instance – but Atwood strongly critiques this cosy notion. The women of Gilead are in the main bitter, resentful and envious, constantly bickering, betraying or jealously watching one another – Commander Fred's household is a perfect microcosm of this.

Context

Radical feminist writer Andrea Dworkin (1946-2005) gained national fame for favouring the anti-pornography movement. In *Pornography: Men Possessing Women* (1981), Dworkin theorised that porn leads to violence by encouraging men to consume media texts that present the abuse of women as erotic entertainment. Like Offred's mother, Dworkin was prominent in the 'Reclaim the Night' protest marches of the late 1970s and '80s, which highlighted the increased violence against women that made many frightened to go out after dark. These issues and ideas were still very current when Atwood was writing *The Handmaid's Tale*.

Context

The Bonfire of the Vanities was the iconic and infamous public destruction by fire of a huge range of allegedly sinful artefacts by the hardline Catholic priest Girolamo Savonarola in Florence in 1497. Savonarola and his followers rounded up and burned items - such as mirrors, make up, clothes, artworks, playing cards and musical instruments - that were seen as frivolous trivialities that could tempt the unwary into evil.

If Offred had been Luke's first wife, she might have been classified as an Econowife within the theocracy. It is unlikely that he would have been seen as being of sufficiently high social status to be recognised as a Commander and therefore assigned a Martha and a Handmaid. As it is, being the fertile second wife of a divorced man means Offred is seen as ideal Handmaid material.

Although the lifelong monogamous (heterosexual) partnership is fetishised within the theocracy, in reality the only Gileadean marriage described in detail – that of Commander Fred and Serena Joy – is riven with jealousy and mistrust. Chapter 34 reveals the hollow sham of a marriage in which love has no place when the Commander justifies the Gileadean system of arranged marriage and subdivided roles for women. He offers an awkwardly compelling quasi-feminist critique of the ways in which modern society has failed to solve all the problems associated with gender equality. 'We've given them more than we've taken away,' he claims. He reminds Offred of the desperate lengths some women felt forced to go to in the time before the establishment of the republic in order to fit in with the unrealistic norms of beauty imposed by mass culture. 'Don't you remember the singles bars … The meat market. Some of them were desperate, they starved themselves thin or pumped their breasts full of silicone, had their noses cut off. Think of the human misery' (Atwood 1996: 231). In the old days (that is, the late twentieth century), he continues:

> [a woman] could be left with a kid, two kids, the husband might just get fed up and take off, disappear, they'd have to go on welfare. Or if they had a job, the children in daycare or left with some brutal ignorant woman, and they'd have to pay for that themselves, out of their wretched little paycheques. Money was the only measure of worth, for everyone, they got no respect as mothers. No wonder they were giving up on the whole business. This way they're protected, they can fulfil their biological destinies in peace. With full support and encouragement.
>
> (Atwood 1996: 231)

This section of the text poses several deliberate challenges to many readers, since Commander Fred's views cannot simply be dismissed out of hand. Most of us would agree that fathers should not be able to abandon their children and clear off scot-free, that women who work should be paid a living wage that allows them to afford high-quality childcare and that mothers who choose to stay at home to raise their children should be valued and supported. According to the Commander, in subdividing the roles of Gileadean women, the Republic has resolved these issues. 'Now tell me,' he challenges Offred (and of course, by implication, the reader), 'You're an intelligent person, I like to hear what you think. What did we overlook?' (Atwood 1996: 231).

From his point of view, the patriarchal structure of the theocracy has engineered these social problems out of existence. Offred's counter-argument for what they overlooked is simple: 'Love, I said' (Atwood 1996: 231). For all its flaws, the imperfect, messy and uncertain world before Gilead – in which people constantly tripped, stumbled and fell – offered freedom. '"Those years were just an anomaly, historically speaking," the Commander said, "just a fluke."' In making the institution of marriage a way of controlling human nature to secure the future of the state, he concludes, 'All we've done is return things to Nature's norm' (Atwood 1996: 232).

'Nothing changes instantaneously: in a gradually heating bathtub you'd be boiled to death before you knew it,' Offred muses (Atwood 1996: 66). Atwood poses tough questions about the metamorphosis from the 'freedom to' that existed in pre-Gileadean days, to the 'freedom from' of the overt and covert misogyny of a patriarchal culture. Put simply, life in Gilead may be seen as less risky for women in some respects, but only because they have been robbed of autonomy and power. Yet when Offred is forced to watch pornographic films showing extreme sexual violence against women, the reader is uneasily aware that life before Gilead was no picnic for the female population either.

Especially sinister is the way in which the theocracy tries to oppress women by taking away their ownership of their own bodies. Aunt Lydia expresses her disgust at the behaviour of women in pre-Gileadean days, explicitly suggesting that their unguarded behaviour incited men to want sex, or perhaps even to go as far as to commit acts of sexual violence. She describes 'The spectacles women used to make of themselves. Oiling themselves like roast meat on a spit, and bare backs and shoulders, on the street, in public, and legs, not even stockings on them, no wonder those things used to happen. *Things*, the word she used when whatever it stood for was too distasteful or filthy or horrible to pass her lips. A successful life for her was one that … excluded *things*. Such *things* do not happen to nice women' (Atwood 1996: 65). Moreover, the language of violence against women extends even to Offred's narrative, which is described as if it were a dismembered corpse. 'I'm sorry that there is so much pain in this story,' says Offred; 'I'm sorry it's in fragments, like a body caught in crossfire or pulled apart by force … this sad and hungry and sordid, this limping and mutilated story' (Atwood 1996: 279).

Women's clothing and costume

The uniquely symbolic and resonant clothing of the Gileadean women, especially that of the Handmaids, can be linked to the debate today about the veiling of Muslim women. By wearing the hijab or niqab, women can prevent themselves being sexually objectified by complete strangers, while retaining the right to unveil at home, in private, at a time of their own choosing. But what if women had no choice but to wear the veil? What if they were forced to do so by men? In the 1970s, some feminists advocated living in single-sex communities, in which the diverse roles and responsibilities of women were chunked up to spread the load and share the pressure; the fragmentation and division of the women of Gilead in their colour-coded uniforms is one not-too-illogical extension of this concept. According to Aunt Lydia, Offred remembers, 'we were a society dying of too much choice' (Atwood 1996: 35).

Atwood's description of Offred and her fellow Handmaids on their way to the Prayvaganza is especially striking:

> I glide with Ofglen along the sidewalk; the pair of us, and in front of us another pair, and across the street another. We must look good from a distance: picturesque, like Dutch milkmaids on a wallpaper frieze, like a shelf full of period-costume ceramic salt and pepper shakers, like a flotilla of swans or anything that repeats itself with at least minimum grace and without variation. Soothing to the eye, the eyes, the Eyes, for that's who this show is for. We're off to the Prayvaganza, to demonstrate how obedient and pious we are.
>
> (Atwood 1996: 224)

The uniforms, of course, make the Handmaids appear to be exactly what they're not. Neither obedient nor pious, Ofglen works for the underground resistance movement and Offred is having a dangerous secret affair with her Commander. The image created here of an endless line of paired and seemingly identical Handmaids suggests that, like Offred and Ofglen, each pair may be harbouring its own secrets.

Atwood has described the hugely symbolic and important robes that identify the different groups of Gileadean women as having a hybrid provenance.

> *The women … wear outfits derived in part from nuns' costumes, partly from girls' schools' hemlines, and partly – I must admit – from the faceless woman on the Old Dutch Cleanser box, but also partly from the chador [an open cloak worn by many Middle-Eastern women when in public, which has no armholes or fastenings and is simply held closed at the front] I acquired in Afghanistan and its conflicting associations. As one character says, there is freedom to and freedom from. But how much of the first should you have to give up to assure the second? All cultures have to grapple with that, and our own – as we are now seeing – is no exception. Would I have written the book if I'd never visited Afghanistan? Possibly. Would it have been the same? Unlikely.*

(Atwood 2005: 207)

▲ The Old Dutch Cleanser box, as advertised on the back cover of the May 18, 1918 Saturday Evening Post

In Gilead women are policed both internally (reading is forbidden and can result in a guilty Handmaid having her hand cut off if discovered) and externally (a peculiarly strange and restrictive dress code is enforced). In Chapter 22 of the novel, Offred remembers Moira's Houdini-like escape from the Red Centre, which involved daringly taking Aunt Elizabeth hostage and then using her security pass to leave, right under the noses of the guards. Dressing up as one of the Aunts is a performative act that demonstrates Moira's categorical refusal to be defined by the Gileadean theocracy. For many readers the true heroine of *The Handmaid's Tale*, Moira is the only character who dares openly to challenge the regime, and her theft of Aunt Elizabeth's uniform and pass is a highly symbolic act of resistance. When we meet her later, wearing the very different uniform of the sexualised Playboy Bunny at Jezebel's, the illicit nightclub-cum-brothel patronised by the Commanders of Gilead, Atwood invites us to study closely Moira's use of costumes to cloak and obscure her identity.

The scenes that take place within Jezebel's are crucially important in terms of Atwood's presentation of gender and power. Within them, we see how she 'raises issues about censorship, and uses camp and kitsch to illustrate certain kinds of freedom – the ability to make personal choices, for example – yet Gilead's leaders understand that recycling a culture cleansed of its playfulness and radical potential will help control a fearful population', as Lorna Irvine notes (Irvine, in Nischik 2000: 209–10). The Jezebel's episode underscores the importance of clothing and once again shows that 'Context is all'. Trashy cheap costumes 'recycled from a freer time [seem] out

Top ten quotation

of place and therefore erotic and radical – old-fashioned lingerie, baby-doll pyjamas, every kind of bathing suit, and exercise and cheerleading outfits' (Irvine, in Nischik 2000: 209–10). When Offred encounters Moira at Jezebel's, dressed in that absurd and symbolically ill-fitting Playboy Bunny outfit, Irvine notes, 'she simultaneously parodies the demeaning nature of the female outfits in Hugh Hefner's former bunny clubs, while she also stands for the irrepressible return of everything the Republic has attempted to obliterate' (Irvine, in Nischik 2000: 210).

Atwood invites us to think about a fascinating intertextual link when Professor Pieixoto points out that Offred's story 'was not a manuscript at all when first discovered, and bore no title. The superscription "The Handmaid's Tale" was appended to it by Professor Wade, partly in homage to the great Geoffrey Chaucer' (Atwood 1996: 313). Chaucer's *Canterbury Tales*, a collection of narrative poems written in the late 1300s, like *The Handmaid's Tale*, dramatises how ordinary people live in a world dominated by religion, with the General Prologue introducing a motley crew of pilgrims – of whom just two are female – on their way to the shrine of St Thomas in Canterbury.

Alyson, the fat-bottomed gap-toothed Wife of Bath, wears an enormous 'coverchief' (wimple or headdress) of fine linen that weighs in at 'ten pound', topping off this astonishing fashion statement with a hat as wide as 'a bokeler or a targe' (a shield or an archery target), scarlet stockings and a 'paire of spores sharpe'. Five times married and a seasoned independent traveller, Alyson can be seen as a proto-feminist within an entirely male-dominated society.

▲ The Prioress, copy of woodcut from the Caxton's Edition of 1485

Meanwhile, the other female pilgrim, the elegant Prioress, with her pretty nose, eyes 'gray as glass' and small, soft, red mouth, has chosen an interesting name for a nun; rather than styling herself Sister Mary or Mother Elizabeth, 'Eglentine' suggests the heroine of a courtly romance. Her 'fair forehead', the epitome of medieval beauty, 'almost a spanne broad', should, of course, be completely invisible underneath her beautifully pleated wimple. Chaucer's description of her stylish coral bracelet decorated with 'beades, gauded all with green' and gold brooch bearing the enigmatic inscription 'Amor vincit omnia' (Love conquers all), should make us question her priorities. Six hundred years later, Margaret Atwood makes the robes worn by the Handmaids of Gilead equally suggestive and symbolic of their complex Madonna/Magdalene role within the theocracy.

The Handmaids' dress is highly stylised, bizarrely contradictory and full of mixed messages. In some ways their robes seem to combine aspects of the Wife of Bath's statement scarlet outfit and the Prioress' habit. 'In Elizabethan days a "nunnery" was another word for a brothel so it is ironic that the Handmaids, whose entire purpose is to reproduce, are expected to wear the white winged headdresses of nuns in extreme orders, and long red dresses and red shoes which both suggest blood, and the traditional idea of a scarlet or loose woman,' suggests Gina Wisker (Wisker 2010: 13). Offred sees herself as a 'distorted shadow, a parody of something, some fairytale figure in a red cloak … A Sister,

Context

The associations of the colour red are disturbing. Culturally, the passing of blood in terms of menstruation and childbirth has often been seen as unclean, with some cultures insisting that women should be 'churched' or purified after childbirth. For the Handmaids of Gilead, of course, menstrual blood is a sign of having failed in their duty of getting pregnant, while childbirth is a triumphant vindication of this.

dipped in blood', also as a 'red shape at the edge of my own field of vision, a wraith of red smoke' (Atwood 1996: 19; 219). In her robes she is identity-less, insubstantial and identical to all the other Handmaids. Their red robes 'incongruously resemble religious habits; their faces are obscured by peaked hats which also function to prevent their seeing anything but what lies immediately in front of them. They are, in fact, personifications of a religious sacrifice, temple prostitutes doomed to a kind of purdah in perpetuity', as Barbara Hill Rigney suggests (Hill Rigney 1987: 117). Offred describes her clothing thus:

> I get up out of the chair, advance my feet into the sunlight, in their red shoes, flat-heeled to save the spine and not for dancing. The red gloves are lying on the bed. I pick them up, pull them onto my hands, finger by finger. Everything except the wings around my face is red: the colour of blood, which defines us. The skirt is ankle-length, full, gathered to a flat yoke that extends over the breast, the sleeves are full. The white wings too are prescribed issue; they are to keep us from seeing, but also from being seen. I never looked good in red, it's not my colour.

(Atwood 1996: 18)

▶ Offred in her robes, from the Poul Rouders English National Opera

Compare the uniforms Commander Fred is suspected to have designed to define and underscore the role of the Handmaid with the costumes worn by the women at Jezebel's, which he clearly finds extremely erotic:

> The women … are tropical, they are dressed in all kinds of bright festive gear. Some of them have on outfits like mine, feathers and glister, cut high up on the thighs, low over the breasts. Some are in olden-days lingerie, shortie nightgowns, baby-doll pyjamas, the occasional see-through negligée. Some are in bathing suits, one-piece or bikini; one, I see, is wearing a crocheted affair, with big scallop shells covering the tits. Some are in jogging shorts and sun halters, some in exercise costumes like the ones they used to show on television, body-tight, with knitted pastel legwarmers. There are even a few in cheerleaders' outfits, little pleated skirts, outsized letters across the chest.

> (Atwood 1996: 246–7)

One of the most troubling descriptions of Offred in the novel is that of her preparing to have sex with the Commander in a hotel room after their visit to Jezebel's:

> I'm a wreck. The mascara has smudged again, despite Moira's repairs, the purplish lipstick has bled, hair trails aimlessly. The moulting pink feathers are tawdry as carnival dolls and some of the starry sequins have come off. Probably they were off to begin with and I didn't notice. I am a travesty, in bad makeup and someone else's clothes, used glitz.

> (Atwood 1996: 265–6)

As Commander Fred prepares to undress her, the image the reader has of Offred is of a broken doll or wounded animal. 'He pulls down one of my straps, slides his other hand in among the feathers, but it's no good, I lie there like a dead bird' (Atwood 1996: 267). Atwood uses the narrator's tragi-comic costume as the objective correlative of her relationship with the Commander here, juxtaposing this scene with the feelings she expresses later, when making love to Nick. 'For this one I'd wear pink feathers, purple stars, if that were what he wanted; or anything else, even the tail of a rabbit,' she declares. 'But he does not require such trimmings' (Atwood 1996: 281). Perhaps the greatest irony here is that the Commander is fully aware of the central importance of dress within any culture; indeed he tries to explain and justify the male desire to play the field and have more than one sexual partner by referring to the female passion for clothes. '**Nature demands variety for men,**' he claims. '**Women know that instinctively. Why did they buy so many different clothes, in the old days? To trick the men into thinking they were several different women. A new one each day**' (Atwood 1996: 249).

Top ten quotation

TASK

The poet and critic T.S. Eliot coined the term 'objective correlative' to describe the way in which objects, situations or events can be used in literature to represent characters or emotions. How far do you agree that the two diametrically opposed outfits worn by Offred — her Handmaid's uniform and the costume the Commander makes her wear to Jezebel's — can be seen as objective correlatives for her fractured identity?

Politics and the environment

When writing *The Handmaid's Tale*, Margaret Atwood, a politically aware and committed writer who has worked for Amnesty International and supports the Green Party of Canada, thought deeply about the political context she was establishing in her future world. In shaping the nightmare Republic of Gilead, she found herself asking 'If you wanted to take over the United States and set up a totalitarian government, the lust for power being what it is, how would you go about it? What conditions would favour you, and what slogan would you propose, what flag would you fly that would attract the necessary 20 per cent of the population, without which no totalitarianism can stay in power?' Her answer was to return to the past and look back three and a half centuries to the iconic theocracy that some see as having built America. 'In this country you'd be … likely to try some version of the Puritan Fatherhood if you wanted a takeover. That would definitely be your best plan' (Atwood 2005: 98). She has also noted that, historically, dictatorships tend to have emerged in bad times, when frightened people will turn to any apparently 'strong leader' who looks likely to fix things, and in *The Handmaid's Tale* the bad times come along as a result of 'a period of widespread environmental catastrophe' which has had the following results:

> …a higher infertility and sterility rate due to chemical and radiation damage (this, by the way, is happening already) and a higher birth-defect rate, which is also happening. The ability to conceive and bear a healthy child would become rare, and thus valued; and we all know who gets the most — in any society — of things that are rare and valued. Those at the top. Hence my proposed future society, which, like many human societies before it, assigns more than one woman to its favoured male members.

> (Atwood 2005: 98)

In terms of the environment, Atwood is equally powerfully engaged. Writing of the early 1960s in the *Guardian* in 2012, she notes:

> Those were less cynical times: people still trusted large corporations. Cigarette brands were still cosy household names, sponsoring such beloved figures as radio's Jack Benny; Coca Cola was still a synonym for wholesomeness, with white-gloved maidens sipping it with their pure lips. Chemical companies were thought to be making life better every

day, in every way, all over the world, which – to be fair – in some ways they were. Scientists in their white coats were presented as crusaders against the forces of ignorance and superstition, leading us forward under the banner of Discovery. Every modern scientific innovation was 'progress' or 'development', and progress and development were always desirable, and would march inevitably onward and upward: to question that belief was to question goodness, beauty and truth.

(Atwood 2012)

Her research was intensive. 'I kept a scrapbook with clippings from newspapers referring to all sorts of material that fitted in with the premises on which the book was based – everything from articles on the high level of PCBs [polychlorinated biphenyls – chemical compounds used to make plastics and in other manufacturing processes] found in polar bears, to the biological mothers assigned to SS troops by Hitler, in addition to their legal wives, for purposes of child production, to conditions in prisons around the world, to computer technology, to underground polygamy in the state of Utah. There is, as I have said, nothing in the book without a precedent' (Atwood 2005: 100).

Context

Margaret Atwood has written powerfully about the impact of Rachel Carson's ground breaking environmental study *Silent Spring* (1962), which exposed the major toxic impact of the widespread use of chemicals to aid pest and disease control. Atwood admires Carson's skill as a writer as well as her scientific expertise, commenting that 'she knew how to explain science to ordinary readers in a way that they could understand; she knew also that if you don't love a thing you won't save it, and her love for the natural world shines through everything she wrote.'

TASK

Read Atwood's article on Carson's *Silent Spring* (listed in the Bibliography on p.102) to gain an excellent insight into Atwood's own ideas about environmentalism and green politics.

The Handmaid's Tale minutely analyses power relationships on both a personal (micro) and more widely socio-political (macro) level. The phrase **'Context is all'** echoes within the text (Atwood 1996: 145). The boundaries between the personal and the political become increasingly blurred, since the Republic of Gilead has more or less conflated the two. Handmaids are concubines, **'two-legged wombs'**, defined purely by their capacity to reproduce; this extreme version of a traditionally patriarchal society actually follows the rules of a typical patriarchal family.

> Top ten quotation

> Top ten quotation

Once, Offred would have seen playing Scrabble as hopelessly old-fashioned – 'the game of old women, old men' (Atwood 1996: 148) – but when played in secret with Fred, her Commander, in a world where the written word is under extreme threat, this innocuous board game acquires an illicit and sexualised thrill. Now that women are forbidden to play Scrabble, the pastime has become edgy and dangerous; 'something different ... desirable ... It's as if he's offered me drugs' (Atwood 1996: 148). Offred becomes increasingly conscious of the many ways in which she sees the world very differently and how quickly the outrageous becomes the everyday.

Religious fundamentalism

'What is needed for a really good tyranny is an unquestionable idea or authority,' Margaret Atwood has written.

Taking it further ▶▶

Research the events that Atwood mentions here, and see how far aspects of the Gileadean regime may mimic real-life historical events.

Political disagreement is political disagreement; but political disagreement within a theocracy is heresy, and a good deal of gloating self-righteousness can be brought to bear on the extermination of heretics, as history has demonstrated, through the Crusades, the forcible conversions to Islam, the Spanish Inquisition, the burnings at the stake under the English queen Bloody Mary, and so on through the years.

(Atwood 2005: 97)

▶ The Salem witch trials

Atwood's critique of extreme religious fundamentalism rests upon her knowledge of the earliest history of the first white settlers in America, the group of English Puritans who became known as the Pilgrim Fathers. The 1620 voyage of the merchant ship Mayflower fostered the iconic myth of a group of religious refugees wanting 'freedom from' oppression and persecution back in England. In reality what they resented was their lack of 'freedom to' oppress and persecute everyone who did not share their extreme version of the Christian faith. Setting the novel in Cambridge, Massachusetts, is another sly reference to the Puritans; as well as being the location of Harvard University, a symbol of research, education and enlightenment, Cambridge is where the notorious Salem witch trials took place in 1692–93. This infamous example of how mass hysteria, extreme religious fervour, jealous score-settling and cruel scapegoating led an enclosed, defensive and inward-looking society to virtually destroy itself, foreshadows the eventual downfall of the Gileadean theocracy.

It is important to remember that Offred herself participates in a Particicution, in which a fearsome group of avenging Handmaids, egged on by Aunt Lydia, tears a man to shreds.

Context

```
This most religious of societies encourages its women
to behave just as the avenging maenads do in the Greek
playwright Euripides' classical drama The Bacchae, which
dates from four centuries BC. In this tragedy, maddened
women, inspired by the god Dionysus and led by King
Pentheus' mother Agave, literally rip Pentheus apart before
destroying the city of Thebes. By alluding to The Bacchae,
Atwood's description of the Particicution may suggest that
any society that encourages such hideous violence will
itself end in destruction.
```

There are clear intertextual links between Atwood's tale of women living within an oppressive theocracy and classic works by the great American writers Nathaniel Hawthorne and Arthur Miller. Set in Puritan Boston in 1642, Hawthorne's 1850 novel *The Scarlet Letter* is the story of Hester Prynne, who is forced to wear a scarlet letter A at all times to publicly brand her an adulteress. Although she is put under intense pressure to name the father of her illegitimate daughter, Hester refuses. The novel tells of the years of cruelty, suffering and humiliation that she suffers for transgressing the sexual code that obtains within the narrow-minded and judgemental Bostonian theocracy. The novel is saturated with biblical language and imagery, and in dealing sympathetically with the then-taboo subjects of sex outside marriage and the birth of an illegitimate child, Hawthorne was way ahead of his time. The parallels between Hester and Offred – both attractive young mothers with a single beloved daughter who are exposed to the jealous cruelty of other women living within a rigidly puritanical culture – are clear.

Interestingly, while Margaret Atwood plays with time by setting *The Handmaid's Tale* some time in the future (in order to make telling points about the present), both Nathaniel Hawthorne and the great mid-twentieth-century playwright Arthur Miller take the opposite approach by setting their fictions in the distant past. Despite its historic setting during the Salem witch trials of 1692 and 1693, Miller's classic drama *The Crucible* (1953) was instantly recognised by his contemporaries as an allegory of the anti-Communist witch-hunts of the day, when the American government blacklisted those suspected of being sympathetic to the Russians. The play's manipulative and spiteful antagonist, Abigail Williams, uses the superstitious fears of the Puritan community to gain

▲ Demi Moore as Hester Prynne in 'The Scarlet Letter' (1995)

49

her revenge on those she despises or resents, eventually accusing Elizabeth Proctor of witchcraft as part of her plan to marry the man she loves, Elizabeth's husband John. As John Proctor himself knows only too well, Abigail is out to destroy her rival. When confessing to having had an affair with Abigail, Proctor cries out in despair, 'A man may think God sleeps, but God sees everything, I know it now. I beg you, sir, I beg you – see her for what she is. … She thinks to dance with me on my wife's grave! And well she might, for I thought of her softly. God help me, I lusted, and there is a promise in such sweat. But it is a whore's vengeance' (Miller 1953). The seething sexual tension between Abigail, John and Elizabeth can be fruitfully compared with the classic triangular relationship between Offred, the Commander and Serena Joy in *The Handmaid's Tale*.

Taking it further ▶

Read or watch a film version of either *The Scarlet Letter* or *The Crucible*, and research the background to your chosen text. What connections can you find between the presentation of Puritanism in this text and in *The Handmaid's Tale*?

Context

▲ Tammy Faye Bakker on the PTL (Praise the Lord) television programme in 1989

At the peak of their popularity in the 1980s, the American televangelist Jim Bakker presented a religious programme called *The PLT* (i.e. 'Praise the Lord') *Club* with his singer and talkshow-host wife, Tammy Faye. According to Tammy Faye Bakker's obituary in *The Telegraph*, 'they collaborated in a ministry of spectacular vulgarity until he was defrocked for adultery and financial mismanagement and jailed on 24 counts of fraud and conspiracy'. Some commentators felt that the initials 'PLT' actually stood for 'Pass the Loot'. Tammy Faye's emotional performances involved dissolving into floods of tears as she sang hymns and said prayers. In the Historical Notes, Professor Pieixoto points out that Commander B. Frederick Judd's Wife was called Bambi Mae; surely this is an Atwood joke at the expense of Tammy Faye? Is it also possible that in her singing career the now dour Serena Joy might have had something of Tammy Faye about her?

Storytelling and mythmaking

Storytelling is a major theme within *The Handmaid's Tale* because the text is a **postmodernist** metanarrative – that is, a story about telling a story.

The novel can be seen as **metafictional** because of the way in which it draws attention to how texts work. Its structure is complex, fragmented and non-linear, and directly reflects on the nature, possibilities and limitations of the act of storytelling itself. Deeply and passionately engaged with essential history, autobiography and narrative practices, the text debates the essential idea of who gets to tell their story. The reader has to rely on Offred's recollection of events, saved, transcribed and archived as it has been by a male authority figure who is far from convinced that her story can add much to his academic reassessment of the history of Gilead. How far does Pieixoto having transcribed and edited Offred's narrative undermine the reader's faith in its authenticity?

The Handmaid's Tale places a female narrator at the centre of the text and deals head-on with issues that impact directly upon women's lives. We see Gilead through Offred's eyes, as if similarly restricted to the view offered by her strange peaked headdress. As Gina Wisker notes, 'everything we are told – even by individuals producing diaries about their lives, as with Offred – is always reconstructed and somewhat fictional, because they are always looking back, reflecting, shaping it for themselves and for any reader to come' (Wisker 2010: 36). With her deep interest in the links between language and identity, it is not surprising that Atwood uses so many aspects of myth, metaphor, symbolism, irony, iconography and allegory. The religious connotations of The Rachel and Leah Re-education Centre, the Aunts, the Prayvaganzas and the Salvagings tap into ideas with which we are culturally familiar.

Context

The literary critic Northrop Frye (1912-91) taught Margaret Atwood when she was an undergraduate student at the University of Toronto. Frye's critical approach focused on the underlying typicality, or archetype, embedded within a literary text. He argued that as creative artefacts, works of literature piggyback on more ancient forms of imaginative experience, such as myths, legends and folk tales, and that the act of 'passing on' mythology recycles narrative modes, patterns, symbols and genres. This allows texts to transcend time, despite the importance of the specific social, cultural and historical context in which they were produced.

Postmodern literature tends to make deliberate use of unusual, hyper-real and deliberately unrealistic narrative strategies that are, by definition, 'made up' in order to raise questions about the relationship between fiction and reality. Metafictional texts constantly remind the reader that what they are experiencing is purely imaginary and challenge the very idea that literature is at its best when it is most 'realistic', in order to destabilise the idea that there is any one clear 'meaning' in any text.

The reader is forced to jigsaw together Offred's jumbled subjective experiences from a patchwork of interrupted memories. We participate in the construction of a coherent narrative comprising of three distinct phases in her life – the time before the Gileadean revolution, her Handmaid training in the Red Centre, and her life in Commander Fred's house – before Professor Pieixoto imposes his ostensibly objective anthropological reading. Perhaps it is because we have already interpreted and reconstructed Offred's story that the Historical Notes come as such a shock; many readers find it hard to accept his detached and impersonal academic stance. As Coral Ann Howells has wryly pointed out, 'By an irony of history, it is Offred the silenced Handmaid who becomes Gilead's principal historian when that oral "herstory" is published two hundred years later' (Howells 2006: 165).

Context

In her later novel *Alias Grace* (1996), Atwood fictionalises an infamous real-life Canadian murder case from 1843, in which the teenager Grace Marks and her fellow servant were convicted of killing their employer and his housekeeper. Throughout the novel the unreliability of Grace's first person narrative is stressed as she provides a range of explanations and motives for her actions. A similar metafictional technique can be seen in Offred's story, although the setting of *The Handmaid's Tale* is, of course, in the near future, as the novel emerges from Atwood's take on the key cultural crises of the 1980s.

One particularly rich irony is that in her former life, Offred worked in a library, 'transferring books to computer disks, to cut down on storage space and replacement costs, they said' (Atwood 1996: 182). Yet the net result of her efforts was to render the books themselves redundant; after being transferred 'they were supposed to go to the shredder' (Atwood 1996: 182). According to Barbara Hill Rigney, Atwood's 'narrative games ... continue to be a contest between reader and author, of, to parody Atwood herself, "who can say what to whom and get away with it."' (Rigney, in Nischik 2000: 164).

In a world where women are forbidden to read shop signs, let alone erotic literature, the act of reading becomes in and of itself something that possesses a forbidden – almost sexual – thrill. In Gilead, Commander Fred has to translate the famous mock-Latin phrase for her, even though the narrator herself once worked with words as a librarian. The narrator's determination to tell her story, even when her memories are blurred, distorted or even manufactured, is the equivalent of Moira's repeated escape attempts and Ofglen's involvement with Mayday. As Rigney notes, Offred's 'responsibility, as it was ... for Orwell's

Winston Smith before his destruction, is to report, to chronicle her time, to warn another world … communication is imperative; she must assume a future audience' (Rigney 1987: 121).

As Howells notes, Offred's story, with its 'confessions of unreliability, challenges Professor Pieixoto's deterministic view of history and the role of historiography as authentication of the past, in favour of something far more arbitrary and subjectively reconstructed' (Howells 2000: 143). Structurally and metaphorically Offred is a liminal figure, hovering on the threshold of Gileadean society and calling into question the criteria by which she is marginalised. The idea that a handful of anthropologists can theorise away or otherwise invalidate the Handmaid's tale makes a mockery not only of the idea that any 'history' can presume to encompass 'herstory' but also the very notion of historical objective truth itself. As even Professor Pieixoto himself admits, we can never really go back:

> We may call Eurydice forth from the world of the dead, but we cannot make her answer; and when we turn to look at her we glimpse her only for a moment, before she slips from our grasp and flees. As all historians know, the past is a great darkness, and filled with echoes.

> (Atwood 1996: 324)

TASK

Professor Pieixoto likens Offred to the mythological character of Eurydice here. Eurydice was so loved by her husband Orpheus that the god Hades took pity on him and allowed him to enter the Underworld to bring her back from the dead, with the sole condition that Orpheus must not turn back to look at her before re-entering the world of the living. At the last moment, Orpheus lost his nerve and turns around, whereupon Eurydice vanished back into the Underworld forever. Discuss the reasons why this mysterious and shadowy figure may be seen as a mirror for Offred.

In revising and subverting various traditional narrative forms and patterns, Atwood not only suggests the problems inherent in getting women's stories heard – let alone valued and validated – but requires us to reflect on the possibilities and limitations of storytelling itself. We have seen how the metafictional 'Historical Notes' that end the novel playfully contest the very notion of written history as documentable and verifiable. As Professor Pieixoto glosses Offred's narrative, Atwood draws attention to the contradictions and complexities of the way in which the Handmaid's tale was produced; far from being a holistic and cohesive document, it is a collated – almost scrapbooked – narrative, transcribed and reconstructed from a pile of old cassette tapes.

Within the literary framework of postmodernism, *The Handmaid's Tale* asks big questions about how we make sense of stories, histories and herstories, and what we then choose to do with them. Pieixoto's critique disputes Offred's ownership of her own experience, challenges the status of her story as a source of narrative truth and denies her the last word on the subject – but then Atwood cunningly (and punningly) has him address a conference at the University of Denay, Nunavit (*deny none of it*). Thus the novel's narrative design seems to reflect the disorienting, uncertain and ambiguous context in which it was originally published thirty years ago; it reminds us that since each text is 'only' one person's view, it can capture 'only' a partial view of things. Typically postmodern (see p.51 for more on postmodernism) in its fragmented non-linear structure and imaginative revisions of a variety of literary modes and elements, *The Handmaid's Tale* reminds us how impossible it is to pin down any one version of the world we live in, but also challenges the very idea that literature – i.e. story telling – is best when it replicates 'real' life.

Target your thinking

- How does Atwood develop her characters as the narrative progresses? (**AO1**)
- What narrative methods does Atwood use to shape the reader's responses to the characters? (**AO2**)

Offred

Formerly a college-educated working wife and mother, the novel's narrator and central protagonist is a Handmaid, a fertile woman whose role is to become a surrogate for an infertile couple who are members of the Gileadean theocracy's elite. As such, her name has been changed to reflect her status as Commander Fred's property; while she remembers her real name – there is a hint that it might be June – she is now known by the state-imposed patronymic 'Offred'. Isolated and virtually friendless, the narrative unfolds entirely from her point of view; we follow her through her day-to-day life as a Handmaid and travel back in time with her as she remembers the time when she lived happily with her husband and young daughter. In many ways, it is a little too simplistic to ask just how heroic the eponymous protagonist is; arguably, the answer may be not at all, since she tends to resist the regime passively and internally as opposed to kicking against it like Moira or joining the resistance like Ofglen. She is pitched midway between Moira the radical rebel and Janine the obedient tell-tale, and while the former disappears and the latter goes mad, Offred, the ordinary heroine, survives. We might well feel that simply enduring the totalitarian nightmare of Gilead for as long as she does is a kind of heroism in itself.

The Commander (Fred)

In many ways the Commander is the most complex and ambiguous character in the novel, since on both a personal and a political level, he represents the very worst of the Gileadean regime. Directly responsible for Offred's oppression, he abuses her for his sexual pleasure and dresses her up like a cheap prostitute; moreover, as a prime mover in the establishment of the Gileadean theocracy, he is equally guilty of exploiting and oppressing *all* women who come within its orbit. Paunchy and middle-aged, the Commander has total control over both his Wife and his Handmaid, yet on a personal level he seems a lonely and rather sympathetic character, far from the stereotypically rigid, unfeeling and cruel patriarch one might expect, given his role as a high-ranking Gileadean military official. Offred neither hates nor fears him and comes to enjoy the evenings she spends reading and playing Scrabble with him in his study.

Imprisoned by the rigid rules he helped to impose upon others, he hypocritically reinterprets them to suit himself in allowing Offred various forbidden privileges. If Professor Pieixoto is right in identifying the Commander as the former market researcher Frederick R. Waterford, then he played a significant role in the establishment of the regime and actually designed the robes worn by the Handmaids. Ironically, therefore, it seems he is ultimately destroyed by the society he founded, when purged by the regime for 'harbouring a subversive'.

Serena Joy

The Commander's deeply unhappy Wife is a complex character. She once presented a religious television programme plugging conservative and anti-feminist social values; ironically, therefore, she was publicly drumming up support for the very patriarchal system that now oppresses her. All women are oppressed and restricted within the confines of the Gileadean theocracy, but despite her privileged position as one of the women with the highest status within the Republic of Gilead, what that actually means for a woman who was once famous in her own right and earned her own living is an existence almost as cramped and confined as Offred's.

Although in Gilead it is always the woman who is branded barren when a couple has problems conceiving, Serena Joy knows or suspects enough to suggest that for Offred to become pregnant, she must sleep with Nick – i.e. someone other than the Commander. In offering to trade a photograph of Offred's daughter for the chance of getting her own baby, Serena Joy reveals not only the extent to which children have become valuable commodities within the Republic but also the complex ways in which powerful women can cruelly oppress less privileged ones. Neither serene nor joyful, she is bitterly jealous of Offred, with whom she discovers her husband is having an illicit sexual relationship that goes well beyond the prescribed limits of the Ceremony. At the end of the novel, it is the Commander's Wife who informs the Gileadean secret police that Offred has broken the rules and must be arrested.

Moira

A college friend of the narrator, funny, vibrant and street-smart, as well as highly educated and politically astute, Moira is something of a heroine to both Offred and the reader; her escape from The Rachel and Leah Re-Education Centre, which involves faking illness before beating up one of the Aunts, is a rare moment of triumph. When Offred visits the state-sponsored brothel, Jezebel's, where Moira works as a prostitute, she learns that Moira chose to be sent there rather than be exiled to the Colonies. Moira's friendship with Offred provides a rare example of female solidarity in a climate that sets women against each other as enemies. As a lesbian, Moira is technically an Unwoman, since heterosexual relationships that can result in pregnancy are the only ones sanctioned by the theocracy. In some ways Moira is prepared to give voice to the forbidden thoughts and feelings that Offred herself is afraid to imagine, and memories of her sexually confident and empowered best friend liberate the narrator from the numbing puritanism of the Republic of Gilead.

Context

The description of Offred's red shoes on page 18 (1996 Vintage), 'flat-heeled to save the spine and not for dancing', when seen in conjunction with Moira's role within the narrative, suggests a possible intertextual link with Moira Shearer, the beautiful red-haired dancer who took the role of doomed ballerina Vicky Page in Michael Powell and Emeric Pressburger's influential film *The Red Shoes* (1948). In the film, Vicky dances the leading role in a ballet based on a Hans Christian Andersen fairy tale of the same name; the cursed red shoes cause the unfortunate girl to dance herself to death. In refusing to wear the Handmaid's robe and shoes, Moira is effectively claiming the right to dance, even if it leads to her ruin.

Nick

The Commander's chauffeur, Nick is a Guardian of the Faithful used as a go-between by both Fred and Serena Joy. Nick's growing emotional bond with Offred is clear from the way she trusts him with her memories of the past as they lie in his bed together. While it is possible that Nick is an undercover Eye, or member of the Gileadean secret police, he may also be working for the underground resistance movement, Mayday. As Atwood has made it clear that Offred does escape at the end of the novel, Nick must be ultimately responsible for saving Offred's life. Critic Barbara Hill Rigney sees Nick as a hero who 'redeems all men by his act of saving Offred, although it may mean his own death. He is a kind of Orpheus to her Eurydice, as he brings her out of the world of the dead' (Rigney, 1987: 119).

Ofglen

The Handmaid 'of/Glen', Ofglen becomes close to Offred as they go shopping together. Eventually Ofglen trusts the narrator enough to admit that she is a member of Mayday, a loosely affiliated rebel group. At the Particicution, Ofglen's apparent fury and violence turns out to be a merciful way of ensuring that the accused rapist, really a fellow rebel, is unconscious before he is torn to pieces. Fearing exposure as an enemy of the state, Ofglen does what many brave rebels do in her position and kills herself before she can betray her confederates or be arrested and exiled. She is then replaced with a far less friendly Ofglen, with whom Offred fails to bond. Like Moira, the original Ofglen is prepared to resist the regime, although in her case she does this by covert and secret means as opposed to Moira's outright rebellion.

Ofwarren (Janine)

Like Offred and Moira, Janine is one of the trainee Handmaids introduced in the very first chapter of the novel. Janine willingly does the bidding of the Aunts, unable to resist the terrible pressure to conform to the norms and values of the Gileadean theocracy. Later renamed Ofwarren, she appears to have achieved every Handmaid's ultimate goal when she gives birth to a baby girl, Angela. Rather than being a healthy Keeper, however, Angela is in fact an Unbaby or Shredder, having been born with an unspecified defect or abnormality. Ofwarren's extremely violent behaviour to the unfortunate scapegoat ripped to pieces during the Particicution suggests that her experiences of living under the Gileadean regime have destroyed her fragile grip on sanity. The fact that the Gileadean system does not bend at all when she has an unhealthy baby would seem to prove that there are no concessions even for good servants of the system.

Aunt Lydia

A senior matron at The Rachel and Leah Re-Education Centre, Aunt Lydia indoctrinates the trainee Handmaids with her clichéd, simplistic, conservative dogma, and also authorises the Handmaids to attack the alleged rapist at the Particicution. She specialises in doing the dirty work of the regime in order to curry favour and retain some authority and status in a world where being an older and infertile single woman offers very limited opportunities. According to Moira, she is a secret sadist masquerading as a faithful and pious servant of the state. Speaking of the way in which Aunt Lydia beat her with a steel cable following her attempted escape, Moira notes, 'She enjoyed that, you know. She pretended to do all that love-the-sinner, hate-the-sin stuff, but she enjoyed it' (Atwood 1996: 260).

Aunt Elizabeth

A minor character, as well as being the Aunt overwhelmed and hogtied by Moira during her escape from the Red Centre, Elizabeth is also the midwife who delivers Ofwarren's baby, Angela.

Luke

Offred's husband seems to have been a kind and decent man who loved his wife and child. Although he is jokingly described as a male chauvinist 'piglet' by his feminist mother-in-law, he does come up with a plan to escape to Canada following the Gileadean assault on women's civil rights. He disappears following the failure of this bid, presumably having been killed by the regime.

TASK

Collate all the textual information that relates to Luke and assess how far he differs from Commander Fred and Nick, the key flesh-and-blood male characters that feature in the text.

Offred's daughter

Offred's daughter, who is now eight years old, was taken away at the age of five after the family's failed escape bid. Serena Joy shows Offred a photograph that proves the little girl has been adopted by an elite Gileadean couple and is being raised as their official Daughter.

Offred's mother

A strong feminist and activist, Offred's mother maintained a warm relationship with both her daughter and son-in-law and protested against pornography and the objectification of women. After the Gileadean theocracy was established, she was labelled an Unwoman and sent to the Colonies; Moira recognised her in a film about those sentenced to this terrible living death of picking over nuclear waste.

The first Offred

The narrator often thinks about her doomed predecessor as Commander Fred's Handmaid, whose relationship with the Commander also went way beyond what is officially sanctioned by the regime. The first Offred hanged herself from the bedroom light fitting when Serena Joy found out about their affair.

Rita and Cora (the Marthas)

While ruling the roost domestically, Serena Joy's cook Rita envies Offred's ability to go shopping. The cleaner, Cora, discovers Offred sleeping in the closet and, having been the person who discovered the Commander's previous Handmaid hanging, fears that Offred will attempt a copycat suicide.

Professor Pieixoto

A Cambridge University academic, Professor James Darcy Pieixoto is the keynote speaker at the Twelfth Symposium on Gileadean Studies, who resurrects and interprets the Handmaid's story two centuries after the fall of the republican regime.

Target your thinking

- How does Atwood develop her themes, settings and characters? (**AO1**)
- What narrative methods does Atwood use to shape the reader's responses as the story unfolds? (**AO2**)

Form and genre

Dystopian fiction

A **dystopia** is an imagined fictional future world straight out of a nightmare. The word comes from the Greek meaning 'not-good place', and was coined by the nineteenth-century philosopher John Stuart Mill as a deliberate inversion of the word **utopia**, a term that since the publication of Sir Thomas More's *Utopia* in 1516 has been commonly used to describe any imagined perfect society.

Texts within the dystopian genre share many classic tropes, which are so commonly recognised as to risk becoming clichéd stereotypes in the hands of a lazy author. Typical motifs include the depiction of a society ruled by a totalitarian government, a complete disregard among the ruling elite for the human rights of the individual, and the aftermath of some kind of epic environmental disaster. (*The Handmaid's Tale* employs all three of these core dystopian themes, of course.) Writers often work within this genre in order to 'forth tell' rather than 'foretell'; in other words they are less concerned with predicting the future than with expressing their worries about the contemporary society in which they live.

'I wanted to try a dystopia from the female point of view – the world according to Julia [the leading female character in Orwell's *Nineteen Eighty-Four*], as it were,' Margaret Atwood has written. 'However this does not make *The Handmaid's Tale* a "feminist dystopia", except insofar as giving a woman a voice and an inner life will always be considered "feminist" by those who think women ought not to have these things' (Atwood 2005: 291). She has described *The Handmaid's Tale* as 'the story of one woman under the regime, told in a very personal way, and part of the challenge for me was the creation of her voice and viewpoint' (Howells 2000: 141). As an example of dystopian fiction, *The Handmaid's Tale* can be seen to reveal what was left out of *Nineteen Eighty-Four*. Whereas George Orwell tells us about the political, military and institutional horrors of his dysfunctional future society, Margaret Atwood describes sex and shopping, childbirth and clothes. The decision to use a female narrator puts an interesting spin on the traditionally masculine form of dystopian fiction, which Coral Ann Howells sees as evidence of Atwood's homing in on both the genre's 'satiric function and on the themes of patriarchal tyranny and absolute social control' (Howells 2000: 141).

Margaret Atwood has spoken and written extensively about the ways in which the network of thoughts came together that inspired her to write *The Handmaid's Tale*. 'I think that, when you have ideas, they come out of a lot of work or experience that you may have done earlier without thinking it was going to lead to that. For instance, at one point in my life, I studied very intensively the American Puritans of the seventeenth century and in another period of my life I read quite intensively a very large number of utopias and dystopias. But I did that many years before. I first read George Orwell's *Nineteen Eighty-Four* when I was fourteen – without thinking, "Now I am going to write a negative utopia." So, what happens, I think, with the creative idea is that a lot of work that you may have done before comes together at a certain point … In other words, you don't have creative ideas about things that you never think about' (Metzler, in Bloom 2001: 279).

Context

In Orwell's *Nineteen Eighty-Four*, the Party's key methods of state control are its four menacing ministries. The names of these government departments sinisterly invert their actual functions, with the Ministry of Peace waging war, the Ministry of Plenty enforcing rationing, the Ministry of Love torturing and brainwashing people, and the Ministry of Truth churning out propaganda.

TASK

As you read *The Handmaid's Tale*, collect evidence of the ways in which the Republic of Gilead tries to adopt similar sinister techniques of state control as in *Nineteen Eighty-Four*.

Speculative fiction

In 1987 *The Handmaid's Tale* won the first Arthur C. Clarke award, given to the best science fiction novel published in the United Kingdom that year. The classification of her novel as 'science fiction' has prompted Margaret Atwood to tease out the essential differences between this and the related genre of 'speculative fiction':

I define science fiction as fiction in which things happen that are not possible today – that depend, for instance, on advanced space travel, time travel, the discovery of green monsters on other planets or galaxies – or that contains various technologies we have not yet developed. But in The Handmaid's Tale, *nothing happens that the human race has not already done at some time in the past, or that it is not doing now, perhaps in other countries, or for which it has not yet developed the technology. We've done it, or we're doing it, or we could start doing it tomorrow. Nothing inconceivable takes place, and the projected trends on which my future society is based are already in motion. So I think of* The Handmaid's Tale *not as science fiction but as speculative fiction; and more particularly that negative form of Utopian fiction that has come to be known as the Dystopia.*

(Atwood 2005: 92–3)

Atwood has differentiated between the events of *The Handmaid's Tale*, which 'invents nothing we haven't already invented or started to invent' and the 'whole other part to the book which is [Offred's] interior monologue. That has to do with the experiencing of and responding to the events rather than the fact itself; it's how the fact feels to a human being' (Atwood 2005: 285; Atwood, in Metzler 2000: 277). It is precisely because Offred remembers the time *before* the Republic of Gilead established its appalling theocratic dictatorship that she is the ideal narrator; indeed this perspective is essential to the telling of her tale.

So let us take a closer look at the most significant elements that Atwood highlights, in an article published in the *Guardian* more than twenty years after *The Handmaid's Tale* was written, as 'some of the things these kinds of narratives can do that socially realistic novels cannot do' (Atwood 2012, see p.101). She points out that speculative fiction can explore new technologies by getting them out of the laboratory or computer suite and into the real world. 'We've always been good at letting cats out of bags and genies out of bottles, we just haven't been very good at putting them back in again … [these] stories in their darker modes are all versions of *The Sorcerer's Apprentice*: the apprentice finds out how to make the magic salt-grinder produce salt, but he can't turn it off' (Atwood 2012). Speculative fiction enables the writer to explore contemporary themes and ideas by pushing them to extremes in a strange but imaginable future context to warn us about the consequences of how we choose to live together. 'As soon as you have a language that has a past tense and a future tense you're going to say, "Where did we come from, and what happens next?" The ability to remember the past helps us plan the future,' Atwood comments (Hoby 2013, see p.102). In *The Handmaid's Tale*, of course, Offred's memories of the time before the establishment of the theocratic dictatorship are critical, providing the most startling points of contrast between the recent past and the reality of the present, as well as a reference point for future historians like Professor Pieixoto.

TASK

In Atwood's 2000 Booker Prize-winning novel *The Blind Assassin*, Iris Chase is in fact the real author of the novel her late sister Laura is famous for having written. Iris is the custodian of Laura's posthumous celebrity, doing the work for which Laura gains all the fame. How might you link this idea to the roles of Offred and Serena Joy?

Slave narrative

The original nineteenth-century slave narratives were the autobiographical accounts of African-Americans who had fallen victim to one of the worst crimes against humanity the world has ever witnessed. *The Handmaid's Tale* is embellished with many of the characteristics of this genre, given that the narrator is treated as a second-class citizen, subject to sexual abuse, deprived of her child and dispossessed of all civil rights. While Offred speaks into a tape recorder, three decades after Atwood's tale of injustice, oppression and resistance within a patriarchal theocracy was first published, the teenage blogger Malala Yousafzai became the youngest ever winner of the Nobel Peace Prize in 2014 for testifying to the oppressive influence of the Taliban in the remote Swat Valley of northwest Pakistan. While the technology may be different, Malala's struggle to tell her story of misogyny, repression and religious injustice still speaks to us all. 'We tell ourselves stories in order to live,' claims cultural commentator Joan Didion in her famous essay 'The White Album' (1979); 'Man is the storytelling animal,' muses Tom Crick, the narrator of Graham

Swift's postmodern novel *Waterland* (1983). *The Handmaid's Tale* also testifies to the potential restorative and therapeutic effects of storytelling, as Offred tries to represent her existence as a narrative rather than a lived experience. Perhaps we might interpret her storytelling as a way of desensitising herself to the horrors of her situation, or of gaining some perspective on it:

> I would like to believe this is a story I'm telling. I need to believe it. I must believe it. Those who can believe that such stories are only stories have a better chance.
>
> If it's a story I'm telling, then I have control over the ending. Then there will be an ending, to the story, and real life will come after it. I can pick up where I left off.
>
> It isn't a story I'm telling.
>
> It's also a story I'm telling, in my head, as I go along.
>
> Tell, rather than write, because I have nothing to write with and writing is in any case forbidden. But if it's a story, even in my head, I must be telling it to someone. You don't tell a story only to yourself. There's always someone else.
>
> Even when there is no one.
>
> (Atwood 1996: 49)

Above all, the text serves to authenticate and legitimise the literary form of the memoir or diary as perhaps the fundamental method of communication for the oppressed.

Romance fiction

In analysing the narrative patterns that link Offred's relationships with Luke, the Commander and Nick, Madonne Miner argues that while the narrator 'wants to imagine these men as unique: Luke as her "real love", husband and father to her child; the Commander as her Gileadean "sugar-daddy" – powerful, distant, in control of her future; Nick as her illicit love, companion in crime', the novel's only significant male characters are in fact eerily similar (Miner, in Bloom 2001: 26).

It is certainly true to say that Luke's reaction to the loss of Offred's post at the library after the Gileadean revolution is, at best, ambivalent; 'It's only a job', he says. Uneasy similarities exist between the nature of Offred's connections with Luke and the Commander; most obviously, her illicit sexual relationships with each of them begin in precisely the same location. The hotel room where she once met Luke when having an affair behind his first wife's back is where the Commander takes her for illicit sex, thus betraying Serena Joy. 'Everything is the same, the very same as it was, once upon a time. The drapes are the same, the heavy flowered ones that match the bedspread, orange poppies on royal blue … All is the same' (Atwood 1996: 263).

In highlighting the fundamental similarity between Offred's lost love and her patriarchal oppressor, Atwood poses uncomfortable questions about the extent to which Luke was ever really the romantic hero the narrator sometimes describes. Even the Commander's chauffeur, Nick, who apparently helps Offred escape at the end of the novel, suppresses her capacity for independent resistance; as Miner notes, 'after Offred begins her affair with Nick, she loses all interest in Mayday and in the possibility of escape … [w]hatever political commitment Offred might be capable of making vanishes in light of her commitment to romance' (Miner, in Bloom 2001: 35). In some ways, it seems, Offred's desire to narrate a romance or fairy story 'closes off other plot options: what would happen if she were to work with Ofglen, to spy on the Commander and communicate his secrets to Mayday?' (Miner, in Bloom 2001: 39).

Structure

When we talk about the structure of a text, we mean the manner in which it is put together. At A-level you need to understand the ways in which the structural aspects of a literary work contribute to and influence our understanding of the text as a whole. While several crucial features of the novel's structure are discussed in the section on pages 51–4, which looks at the theme of storytelling and mythmaking, there are some other key structural devices used by Atwood that you should study in detail.

Movement in time: Night and Day

The Handmaid's Tale, as a typically postmodern text, does not keep moving forward in time chronologically; instead, while the episodes set in Gilead move forward towards the dramatic climax of Offred's arrest, we are also periodically taken back in time to the days before the Gileadean revolution. The clearest demarcations within the novel are between the sections dealing with past and with present – i.e. 'Night' and, we might assume, 'Day'. In the 'Night' sections, Offred often describes past events and memories, some of which include her husband, Luke, and her daughter, while elsewhere in the narrative she describes the daily round of events in her present life as the Commander's Handmaid.

CRITICAL VIEW

Structuralism has been defined as the search for the underlying patterns of thought in all aspects of human life. It involves comparing the relationships between elements in any given system.

Binary opposites, juxtapostioning, patterning and doubling

The concept of binary opposites stems from the work of the French intellectuals Claude Lévi-Strauss (1908–2009) and Roland Barthes (1915–80), who were closely associated with the theory of **structuralism**.

In terms of literary theory, structuralists argue that since the meaning of a word is not actually contained in its name, we tend to construct its meaning by relating each word to its opposite. They characterise words as symbols that signify society's ideas and suggest that meaning emerges from the gap between two opposing concepts; thus in order to grasp an idea such as *masculinity* we refer to its binary opposite, *femininity*. Layers of inferential meaning can emerge when a writer consciously structures a text using core oppositions and patterns like this, and in *The Handmaid's Tale* Atwood makes frequent use of this technique by inviting the reader to consider essential dichotomies (or divisions into separate parts), such as:

- masculinity and femininity
- regeneration and decay
- physicality and spirituality
- present and past
- fertility and sterility.

Inviting the reader to consider similar or contrasting ideas or concepts can shed light on them both. Think about Atwood's reasons for using the structural techniques of juxtapositioning, patterning, doubling and/or foreshadowing in the following examples:

- Offred's sexual encounters as the mistress firstly of Luke and then of the Commander, which take place in the same hotel bedroom.
- The juxtapositioning of Offred's sexual encounters with the Commander and Nick on the same night.
- Janine's two near-identical nervous breakdowns, firstly in the Red Centre and then following the Particicution.
- Offred's view of herself in her Handmaid's uniform and in the costume chosen for her by the Commander on their night out at Jezebel's.
- Moira and Janine as foils; the narrator and the first Offred as doppelgängers.
- The two Offreds and the two Ofglens.

Epistolary fiction

An epistolary novel is comprised of a series of documents, often taking the form of a series of letters exchanged between various characters or of a sequence of diary entries. *The Handmaid's Tale* is perhaps best seen as a text that contains epistolary elements as opposed to a fully-fledged example of the genre, as the individual chapters are reminiscent of entries in an ongoing journal. It is also possible to see the inserted story of Moira's escape as rather like a letter. In handing over narrative control to another person, Atwood can tap into a different viewpoint while not making use of a traditional omniscient narrator. The certainty associated with the all-seeing all-knowing overarching narrative point of view would go completely against the grain of the novel, in which Offred's difficulties with telling her story is one of the most crucial themes.

The Historical Notes

Atwood's decision to switch narrative voices at the end of the book, replacing Offred with the Cambridge academic Professor Pieixoto, comes as a major shock, as a male critic appears to deconstruct the Handmaid's challenge to masculine power and authority. The metafictional Historical Notes that follow Offred's narrative do little to gloss or in any sense finalise the text for the disorientated reader, whatever Professor Pieixoto might think. There is also a thread of detection running through the text, as the central mystery – the solution to which Professor Pieixoto fails to spot, although the attentive reader probably will – is that of the narrator's real name; of the trainee Handmaids mentioned at the start of the novel, only one – June – is not specifically linked with another character as the story develops. Another puzzle is the meaning of the cryptic message hidden by Commander Fred's previous Handmaid. These detective elements add another level of genre interest to an already dazzlingly multifaceted text.

Language

In the Republic of Gilead, as in so many classic dystopian settings, language itself is under threat. Just as the Nazis burned books, knowing well that ignorance serves the purposes of any would-be dictatorship, so within this theocratic totalitarian state, literacy is being slowly eradicated as images replace writing on public signs. In some ways, therefore, *The Handmaid's Tale* is all about the power of language and the problems we have with it; this in a world in which personal power, pleasure and satisfaction can be found in being able to play a simple word game like Scrabble.

The novel's title

Margaret Atwood signals one of the central themes of the text with a deceptively simple yet powerfully evocative title that gets straight to the heart of things. The implications of the word 'Handmaid' neatly encapsulate Offred's predicament as a woman caught in a uneasy and twisted three-way relationship, but it is the connotations of the word 'tale' that are most striking. As well as evoking the idea of a 'fairy tale' – a simple children's story too fantastical to be true – the term taps into our awareness of various negative idioms, such as an 'old wives' tale', meaning a myth or piece of unreliable gossip, or 'telling tales', meaning spitefully getting someone into trouble. It evokes Shakespeare references to 'a tale told by an idiot' in *Macbeth* and seven-year-old Mamillius' astute observation in *The Winter's Tale* that 'a sad tale's best for winter'. As Professor Pieixoto states, it is a label attached to Offred's narrative 'partly in homage to the great Geoffrey Chaucer' (Atwood 1996: 313). Consider this: what difference would be made by changing the novel's title to *The Handmaid's Narrative* or *The Handmaid's History*?

Chapter headings

Chapter titles are sometimes startling in their apparent everyday ordinariness; 'Shopping' or 'Nap', for example. Meanwhile, signs and symbols wobble in and out of focus, as when the reader discovers the mismatch between shopping as they know it and shopping in Gilead, where the brash logos of the typical high street or shopping centre have been replaced by religious pictograms because the Handmaids are forbidden to read.

Names and the naming process

Within Offred's narrative, as Professor Pieixoto points out, no one is identified by their real name; the narrator almost certainly uses pseudonyms to protect others and Ofglen commits suicide rather than 'name names' under torture. But without a name, how can anyone retain a sure grasp on their own identity? We're not even sure we know the narrator's real name; the central protagonist is known only by her patronymic 'Of/Fred', which denotes her status as the Commander's Handmaid. As she declares:

> My name isn't Offred, I have another name, which nobody uses now because it's forbidden. I tell myself it doesn't matter, your name is like your telephone number, useful only to others; but what I tell myself is wrong, it does matter. I keep the knowledge of this name like something hidden, some treasure I'll come back to dig up, one day. I think of this name as buried. This name has an aura around it, like an amulet, some charm that's survived from an unimaginably different past.

> (Atwood 1996: 94)

Heidi Sletterdahl Macpherson has summarised the other ways in which the name *Offred* has been interpreted by various critics: 'she is off-red, or not quite fully aligned with her role; she is offered up; she is off-read, as in mis-read, and she is afraid' (Macpherson 2010: 56). Just as the narrator cannot read the subversive aphorism secretly carved into the wall of her bedroom cupboard by a previous Handmaid, **'nolite te bastardes carborundorum'** meaning 'Don't let the bastards grind you down', so the reader can struggle to decipher Offred's own identity.

> Top ten quotation

Context

In emphasising the power of knowing one's own name, *The Handmaid's Tale* can again be compared with Arthur Miller's *The Crucible*, in which the persecuted hero John Proctor refuses to sign a false confession; he declares, 'Because it is my name! Because I cannot have another in my life! Because I lie and sign myself to lies! … How may I live without my name? I have given you my soul; leave me my name!'

Titles

For the significance of the division of the citizens of the republic into different categories, refer back to the section on pages 3–4 called 'who's who in Gilead'.

Neologisms

In the world of *The Handmaid's Tale*, as also occurs so famously in Orwell's *Nineteen Eighty-Four*, neologisms (new coinages) have entered the language to reflect the new reality of everyday life. Some of the words in the revised Gileadean lexicon are portmanteau words or blends, i.e. 'mash-ups' of existing words that carry a resonant significance in the context of the theocratic dictatorship:

- **Prayvaganza** – a compound word formed from the words 'prayer' and 'extravaganza'. Both these words would seem to have positive connotations, but in the context of Gilead, this word acquires a sinister negative overlay when applied to ostentatious public celebrations.

- **Particicution** – a compound word formed from the words 'participation' and 'execution'. This coinage stresses that the Handmaids are forced into complying with the scapegoating of an outsider, who is killed to solidify the crowd mentality of the in-group.

- **Salvaging** – this term blends the diametrically opposed words 'salvation' and 'savaging' to convey something of the madness inherent in believing that executing someone can in some way save them.

- **Identipasses** – internal passports introduced soon after the Gileadean revolution, which are used to monitor and control the population.

- **Pornycorners** and **Pornomarts** – disparaging terms referring to the omnipresence of brothels, adult shops and other outlets of the sex industry in pre-Gileadean days. They were outlawed soon after the suspension of the Constitution.

- **Feels on Wheels** – a vehicle that provided sexual services before the revolution; these are banned in Gilead. The name is a pun on 'Meals on Wheels' programmes, which cater for elderly or housebound people.

- **Bun-Dle Buggies** – presumably vehicles that conveyed mobile 'prostitutes-to-go' for their clients, these are banned in Gilead. Taken with the Pornycorners, Pornomarts and Feels on Wheels, this term suggests the ubiquity of pornography in the USA before the Gileadean revolution.

- **Compu** – a prefix based on the word 'computer', which is used to form new words with a technological feel to label artefacts such as credit cards, PINs and scanners, etc. For instance, **Computalk**, **Compunumber**, **Compubite**, **Compuphone**, **Compucount** and **Compubank**. After the Republic bans paper money, financial transactions have to be made using a Compunumber, for example.

- **Angel makers** – doctors who performed abortions in pre-Gileadean times.

- **Manhattan Cleanup** – the equivalent of Savonarola's Bonfire of the Vanities, this was the official burning of all clothing that pre-dated the imposition of the coloured uniforms that denote the different types of women.

- **Sons of Jacob Think-Tank** – the in-group who came up with the blueprint for the Gileadean coup and the establishment of the new social order. Its members have named themselves after the patriarch who sired the twelve tribes of Israel with his official wives Rachel and Leah, and their handmaids Bilhah and Zilpah.

- **Gyn Ed** – the Red Centre education programme that teaches the Handmaids how to be (Gileadean) women.

- A highly significant neologism that has clearly emerged under the radar of the official regime is the **Underground Femaleroad** that Moira describes to Offred, which must have been named in homage to the Underground Railroad that helped escaped slaves reach safety in the American Civil War era. It seems extremely unlikely that the regime itself would assign a name with such positive connotations of liberation to a network of safe houses designed to smuggle women northwards towards the Canadian border. To the Gileadean elite, this system would have been seen as a dangerous example of outright treachery. Ironically, in his lecture Professor Pieixoto refers to this network as the **Underground Frailroad**, a further example of his supercilious and patronising humour that indicates a belief in the essential weakness or 'frailty' of women. It also reminds us of Hamlet's denunciation of his mother, Gertrude, upon her remarriage; 'Frailty, thy name is woman!' (Shakespeare 1599–1602: 1:2).

Biblical language

As a theocracy, the Republic is of course steeped in the language of the Bible, which it uses to shore up its norms and values. '**Blessed are the meek**', pontificates Aunt Lydia, but in omitting the important second half of this Beatitude, 'for they shall inherit the earth', she totally distorts Jesus' original message that the oppressed will finally win the day. The Republic that subjugates and oppresses women has called itself Gilead after 'the mountain where Jacob promised his father-in-law, Laban, that he would protect his two daughters (Leah and Rachel)', says Atwood (Atwood 2005: 99). Yet it chooses to pass over the awkward biblical description of Gilead in the Old Testament book of Hosea: 'Gilead is a city of wicked men, stained with footprints of blood' (Hosea 6:4). The fundamentalists of the Republic are frequently engaged in **sect wars** – violent and bloody battles fought against Jews, Jehovah's Witnesses and other religious groups.

Testifying, a term usually associated with a solemn Christian fundamentalist ritual in which the faithful describe how they gave up sin and embraced the love of God, has had its former meaning grotesquely wrestled out of shape in Gilead, where it means admitting to some past crime, real or often made up. At The Rachel and Leah Re-education Centre the trainee Handmaids are expected to admit to past offences, such as illicit sexual activities (and this includes being a victim of rape) or having undergone an abortion, while the Aunts encourage the others to condemn them. The idea is to brainwash the Handmaids into accepting their current situation.

On another occasion Offred recalls the way Aunt Lydia used to have the trainee Handmaids chant a core Gileadean mantra, '*From each according to her ability, to each according to his needs* … It was from the Bible, or so they said. St Paul again, in Acts' (Atwood 1996: 127). But Aunt Lydia is wrong to claim a biblical provenance here; these words are not from the Bible at all. In fact she is misquoting the political philosopher Karl Marx's description of how a perfect communist society will be able to meet the needs of all its citizens, unlike the unequal distribution of wealth that occurs within a capitalist system. Marx described organised state religion contemptuously as 'the opium of the people', meaning it leaves them in a state of stunned passivity and encourages them in the name of God not to rebel against their oppressors; the idea of Aunt Lydia mistakenly parroting his ideas as the equivalent of Holy Writ is downright funny. Beyond this, of course, Aunt Lydia is even distorting Marx's words in using them to vindicate the imbalance of power between men and women in Gilead, rather than accept his original meaning of everyone being provided for equally. On the other hand, the prepositions and pronouns she uses are significant; in this patriarchal theocracy, things are indeed taken *from her* and given *to him*.

The language of the Bible is further seen in the symbolic names given to branded goods and shops. Gileadean cars are given self-consciously archaic biblical names that actually have a comical aspect in their struttingly clichéd 'petrol-head' masculinity; for some readers, **Whirlwinds**, **Chariots** and **Behemoths** might evoke a stifled snigger as opposed to awed respect. The names of the shops are even more significant – especially when, over time, the words on their signs are replaced with pictorial symbols so that the Handmaids are unable to commit the sin of reading while out on their shopping trips. Key examples include:

- ◤ **All Flesh** – the butcher's shop. The name picks up on the biblical warning about 'the way of all flesh'.

- ◤ **Milk and Honey** – the greengrocer's shop. The biblical phrase for a land of plenty – that is, one flowing with milk and honey – is meant to resonate here.

- ◤ **Daily Bread** – the bakery's name stems from the words of the Pater Noster or Lord's Prayer, 'Give us this day our daily bread'.

- ◤ **Loaves and Fishes** – named after Jesus' miraculous feeding of the five thousand, Gilead's fishmonger's shop is hardly ever open, since the sea is so polluted that most fish are too poisonous to eat.

- ◤ **Soul Scrolls** – the prayer shop where the Commanders' Wives buy their prayers in order to advertise the purity of their souls. The soul scrolls themselves are automated machines that enable the Wives to buy prayers remotely and have the cost deducted from their Compucounts.

▼ **Lilies of the Field** – the clothes shop; formerly a cinema. The name derives from Jesus' exhortation to 'Consider the lilies, how they grow: they neither toil nor spin, yet I tell you, even Solomon in all his glory was not arrayed like one of these' (Luke 12:27). The idea that it is far better to leave something (or someone) in its natural and unadorned state is, of course, used in Gilead to justify the banning of make-up for women.

Puns and word play

Atwood knows well this aspect of dystopian fiction.

▼ **Pen Is Envy** – a saying of Aunt Lydia's, this riff on the Freudian psychological term 'penis envy' is designed to warn the Handmaids off the very idea of writing. Sigmund Freud's theory suggests that adolescent girls go through a period of severe psychosexual anxiety when they realise that they do not have a penis; Margaret Atwood is suggesting that what women envy is the power to express themselves in writing.

▼ **Nolite te bastardes carborundorum** – meaning 'don't let the bastards grind you down,' the coded message left behind by the Commander's previous Handmaid becomes a secret mantra for the narrator. It is written as a version of the Latin aphorism 'Non illegitimi carborundum', suggesting that the former Handmaid had not acquired it through official Latin lessons, but in a more informal way.

> Top ten quotation

▼ **There is a Bomb in Gilead** – this is Moira's irreverent rewording of the hymn 'There is a balm [consolation] in Gilead'; clearly within the context of the novel, Moira's version signals her willingness to fight the theocracy using violence if it comes to it (Atwood 1996: 230).

▼ **Nick, the private Eye** – this pun links the Commander's chauffeur with the sauve, charming and debonair film detective Nick Charles, played by William Powell, in a hugely popular series of comic film thrillers that began with *The Thin Man* (1934). Significantly, Nick worked in tandem with his witty and sophisticated wife Nora (Myrna Loy) to fight crime and drink cocktails.

▼ **The University of Denay, Nunavit** – Professor Pieixoto addresses a conference at a university whose very name instructs him not to undermine the essential truth of Offred's narrative – in other words, he (and, by extension the reader) is exhorted to 'deny none of it'.

Images, motifs and symbols

Writers often use related language patterns and clusters to infuse certain characters with particular associations, evoke a specific mood or atmosphere, or to draw attention to a particularly significant theme. In *The Handmaid's Tale* Atwood uses recurring images, motifs and symbols to create a sense of dramatic and structural coherence. You should think about the ways in which the overarching effects of her complex range of images, motifs and symbols enrich the unique atmosphere of the text.

Perhaps the most noticeable imagery clusters within the text are associated with Offred's use of the natural world to create visual stimuli for the reader. These may be seen to function as a kind of feminised language to counterbalance and challenge the harsh rhetoric and crass neologisms perpetuated by the Gileadean regime. One especially noticeable imagery cluster centres on flowers, as their freedom to grow wild provides such a painful contrast with the circumscribed role of Offred herself. Red tulips come to represent the fertility of the Handmaids themselves; very early in the novel Offred notes that 'The tulips are red, a darker crimson towards the stem; as if they had been cut and are beginning to heal there' (Atwood 1996: 22). Serena Joy is a keen gardener, but symbolically as the tulips in her garden open out in their gorgeous crimson lushness, 'the daffodils are now fading' (Atwood 1996: 22). The identification of the Handmaid with the fertile tulip and the Commander's Wife with the dying daffodil is made explicit later on in the novel, when Offred, feeling rebellious, sneaks down to the living room determined to steal a 'magic flower'. The one she settles on, a 'withered daffodil', is to be taken from Serena Joy's vase. 'The daffodils will soon be thrown out, they're beginning to smell. Along with Serena's stale fumes, the stench of her knitting' (Atwood 1996: 109).

Some of the most powerful visual and verbal motifs and symbols that occur in *The Handmaid's Tale* have been discussed elsewhere in this book, in the Chapter summaries and commentaries section (page 5) as well as the Themes section (page 38), but to recap the main ones are listed here:

▼ **Items of clothing** – such as the iconic official Gileadean uniforms and the sexualised costumes of the women at Jezebel's.

▼ **Parts of the human (usually female) body** – such as the eyes, face, skin, hands, feet, breasts, blood and womb.

▼ **Nature's miracles and fertile treasures** – such as eggs, plants, animals, the seasons, light and, of course, flowers.

TASK

Trace and analyse these key imagery clusters and assess the ways in which they serve to highlight Atwood's major themes. If you are working with other students, you might allocate one cluster to each group and then share your findings.

Target your thinking

- What different critical positions might be applied to *The Handmaid's Tale* to extend your knowledge of the text? (**AO1**)
- How can setting *The Handmaid's Tale* within a broad range of contexts deepen your understanding of the text and the ways in which different readers might respond to it? (**AO3**)
- What links might be traced between *The Handmaid's Tale* and various other literary texts? (**AO4**)
- How can applying various critical approaches enrich your understanding of *The Handmaid's Tale* and the ways in which different readers might interpret it? (**AO5**)

Biographical context

Margaret Eleanor Atwood was born on 18 November 1939 in Ottawa, Ontario, Canada, the second of the three children of scientist Carl Atwood and his wife Dorothy. Atwood had an unusual childhood in which she often missed out on formal schooling in order to accompany her father, an entomologist (expert in insects), on his field trips and expeditions. An early, voracious and advanced reader, she explored writing from within genres as diverse as comics, mystery stories and fairy tales. Not until almost the end of the Second World War did Atwood finally begin to live in more conventional city surroundings and to attend school regularly. Having begun to write at the age of just six, she knew she wanted to make it her career even before she went to university.

A prize-winning student, Atwood graduated from the University of Toronto with a degree in English, having taken minors in Philosophy and French. Having been awarded a fellowship to study at Harvard University, her work there with Professor Perry Miller affected her so profoundly that he is one of the dedicatees of *The Handmaid's Tale;* much of the novel is of course set in and around the Harvard campus. Atwood's long-term relationship with the writer Graeme Gibson produced her only child, Eleanor, who was born in 1976.

▲ Margaret Atwood (during an interview in Toronto, 2014)

Atwood has published some important works of literary criticism in which she describes Canadian literature as marked by the themes of survival and victimhood and theorises as to the impact and implications of these key themes on her mother country's writing and culture. She has taught at many universities and been awarded honorary degrees by Oxford, Cambridge and the Sorbonne. Her interest in how history and narrative can entwine and enrich one another can also be seen in some of the novels she has published since *The Handmaid's Tale*, such as *Alias Grace* (1996) and *The Blind Assassin* (2000).

The winner of numerous prestigious literary prizes and awards, Margaret Atwood is a founder member of the Writers' Trust of Canada, which aims to support the writing community of her native country. For her epic contribution to Canadian literature, Atwood was inducted into the national Walk of Fame in 2001. A noted humanist, Atwood believes in human beings as the agents of their own destiny and values rational critical thinking over religious faith; significantly she was named Humanist of the Year by the American Humanist Association soon after the publication of *The Handmaid's Tale*.

TASK

Create a visual representation of the contextual background to *The Handmaid's Tale*. Working with other students, you could design a timeline or wall display to illustrate the key historical, political, social and cultural contexts to which Margaret Atwood was responding.

Political, social and historical contexts

Reaganism

'Reaganism' is the term given to the conservative political and economic ideologies associated with the American President Ronald Wilson Reagan (1911–2004), who dominated global geopolitics throughout the 1980s. A former Hollywood film actor, during his two terms as president, from 1981–89, Reagan implemented a radical plan of conservative reform initiatives, slashing taxes in order to reduce government spending, establishing the so-called War on Drugs, and invading the island of Grenada as part of his fervent anti-communist agenda, even though it was in fact a British Crown Colony. Hugely popular, Reagan won two landslide election victories and the strong personal relationships he formed with Soviet leader Mikhail Gorbachev and British Prime Minister Margaret Thatcher had much to do with the ending of the Cold War. Even today, Reagan remains one of the most widely popular and iconic American Presidents ever, with his conservative agenda now seen as having led to a major shift to the right in American political thinking.

The rise of the conservative religious right

In tandem with the political and economic paradigm shifts engineered by Reagan, various social and cultural changes took place during the 1980s that Margaret Atwood viewed with much disquiet. During the 1980s various right-wing evangelical Christian groups became increasingly vocal in their determination to influence public policy and social attitudes in accordance with their religious beliefs. The Christian right grew exponentially in influence during the 1980s and the advent of televangelism allowed for the widespread dissemination of their socially conservative condemnation of Darwinism, scientific research, homosexuality, divorce, abortion, contraception, obscenity and pornography. The parallels with the Republic of Gilead should be clear.

The 1980s anti-feminist backlash

In 1991, the American writer Susan Faludi published *Backlash: The Undeclared War against American Women*, a study of what she saw as a media-driven wish to turn back the clock following the advances made by feminist campaigners during the 1970s. Faludi suggested that this typically hostile response was an example of the classic knee-jerk historical reaction that reoccurs periodically whenever women seem to have achieved a measure of social equality, status or progress.

Margaret Atwood was intensely concerned with the growing counter-attack against feminism that took place in the 1980s. This was led by conservative social commentators such as Phyllis Schafly who saw the liberation of women as posing a clear threat to 'traditional family values'. In a kind of 'two-steps-forward, one-step-back' dance, just as women seemed to have made some substantial advances in terms of social equality, their achievements were openly criticised by those cultural conservatives who felt endangered by the changes they saw happening around them. Ironically, of course, this anti-feminist retaliation worked on the 'attack is the best form of defence' idea, as a kind of pre-emptive strike designed to stop women in their tracks long before they ever reached their goal of total equality. In a reversal of logic that the Republic of Gilead itself might be proud of, the very changes that had led to women having a fairer stake in society came to be blamed for egging them on to ruin. From this ideological standpoint, abortion and contraception do not liberate women from the fear of having an unwanted child, but instead threaten the very concept of the traditional family. Thus Atwood began to write *The Handmaid's Tale* just at the historical moment when, after women had begun to make obvious sustained progress towards full empowerment, equality and social justice, an all-too-predictable conservative counter-offensive kicked in.

Context

The idea of an 'anti-feminist backlash' is far from new. *The First Blast of the Trumpet Against the Monstrous Regiment of Women* (1558) was the firebrand Calvinist cleric John Knox's notorious polemical attack on what he saw as the obscene situation of three major European countries being ruled by women, namely Elizabeth I of England, Mary Queen of Scots and Catherine de Medici, the Regent of France. Knox argued that allowing female rulers ran contrary to the word of God.

Environmental concerns

After the Second World War and the atomic bombing of Hiroshima, an increasing awareness of the manifold ways in which humanity was putting the planet at risk gradually started to sink in with the general public. Global issues – such as oil spills, climate change, nuclear testing, air pollution, energy problems and the overuse of pesticides – led to a climate of growing public concern. The burgeoning environmental movement galvanised much public support and recognition by staging the same kind of successful protest marches and meetings as had galvanised the civil rights and anti-Vietnam protesters of the 1960s.

Anti-nuclear protests reached a peak in the 1970s and 1980s, with the infamous 1979 meltdown at the Three Mile Island reactor in Pennsylvania – the worst nuclear accident in US history – causing a major public scandal. Unsurprisingly, given the panic induced by this incident, an anti-nuclear rally held in New York's Central Park in 1982 attracted a million demonstrators. In *The Handmaid's Tale*, the pollution that has caused mass infertility in the former USA, now the Republic of Gilead, appears to be national and limited. In *Oryx and Crake* (2003), Atwood escalates her portrayal of environmental Armageddon to a global level, describing a bleak post-apocalyptic world of bioterrorism and catastrophic climate change. As a member of the Green Party of Canada, Margaret Atwood was extremely concerned by the high-profile environmental problems that began to penetrate deep into the public consciousness during the 1980s, and *The Handmaid's Tale* is saturated with echoes of this apprehension.

Literary and cultural contexts

Canadian literature (CanLit)

CRITICAL VIEW

Some would argue that *The Handmaid's Tale* is a work of American literature, since Atwood was living in Massachusetts when she wrote it and since its setting and themes reflect the USA of the 1980s. On the other hand, CanLit critics would argue that overwriting Atwood's identity as a Canadian in order to annex *The Handmaid's Tale* and incorporate it within the canon of American National Literature is an act of cultural imperialism akin to Professor Pieixoto's interpretation of Offred's narrative.

Bordered by the USA to the south, Canada gained full independence from the United Kingdom only in 1982; today it is a key member of the Commonwealth and retains Queen Elizabeth II as official Head of State. When Margaret Atwood was a university student in the late 1950s, 'Canadian literature' as a distinct body of work simply did not exist; today, however, 'CanLit' certainly does exist, and Atwood herself is perhaps its single most important living exponent.

It is well worth thinking about how Atwood uses the Republic of Gilead in *The Handmaid's Tale* to represent the USA, the global superpower that is her mother country's nearest neighbour. The critic David Staines argues that 'Perhaps only a Canadian, a neighbour as well as an outsider to the United States, could create such an unsettling vision of the American future. In implied contrast to Gilead is its northern neighbour, once again the final stop of a new underground railroad, this time one that smuggles handmaids to the freedom of Canada' (Staines, in Howells 2006: 21).

As Gina Wisker has noted, much of Atwood's work:

...concentrates on exploring and rewriting representations of Canada and what it means to be Canadian ... However the themes and concerns of her novels ... are also generalisable to many other locations and contexts, to other societies and places, and so they speak to us as readers whether we are located in the US, Canada, UK, or Australasia, Europe, the Caribbean. The Canadian context is noticeable in The Handmaid's Tale *as Canada features as a place of relative equality and security, while the US has been polluted, has undergone terrible wars and reverted to a version of religious fundamentalism which operates a class system based on fertility or lack of it, and patriarchal power. Considering Atwood as a Canadian writer means recognising*

*the relationship between the US and Canada, where the US is often
seen as a brasher more powerful neighbour and Canada as more liberal
and tolerant, less warlike.*

(Wisker 2010: 6)

The Future Library

As the first contributor to the Future Library project, Margaret Atwood has
recently written a story that will be read only in a century's time, long after her
own death. Her book is the first of a hundred to be written by different authors
between now and 2114; a forest has been planted in Norway and its trees will
be used to make the paper on which the Future Library will be printed. According
to Atwood, 'it goes right back to that phase of our childhood when we used to
bury little things in the backyard, hoping that someone would dig them up, long
in the future, and say, "How interesting, this rusty old piece of tin, this little
sack of marbles is. I wonder who put it there?"' Moreover, she argues, 'when
you write any book you do not know who's going to read it, and you do not know
when they're going to read it. You don't know who they will be, you don't know
their age, or gender, or nationality, or anything else about them. So books … are
like the message in the bottle' (Flood 2014, see p.102).

The young artist in charge of the Future Library, Katie Paterson, argues that the
contributors can write whatever they like 'in any language and any context …
on the theme of imagination and time … I think it's important that the writing
reflects maybe something of this moment in time, so when future readers
open the book, they will have some kind of reflection of how we were living
in this moment' (Flood 2014). No wonder Margaret Atwood was Paterson's
dream first author; the central premise of a woman's words being locked away
to await decryption by readers as yet unborn is, after all, the DNA of *The
Handmaid's Tale*.

Performance context

When studying *The Handmaid's Tale*, watching Volker Schlondorff's 1990 film
version of the text will certainly enhance your ability to engage with the text, as
long as you keep asking yourself what has been gained and what has been lost
in the move from page to screen.

TASK

Watch the final
scene of the 1990
film version two
or three times
and compare it
closely with the
printed text. How
do you interpret
the director's
vision here?

Context

Margaret Atwood's interest in writing and communication led
her in 2004 to invent the LongPen, a remote robotic device
that means that she no longer needs to physically attend
bookshop signings. Using the LongPen, Atwood can see and
hear a person buying her novel thousands of miles away as
she signs their personal copy.

TASK

As you apply different critical positions to *The Handmaid's Tale*, keep a detailed reading diary. Discussing your interpretations with other students can help you to challenge and develop your own ideas.

Critical contexts

Ways of thinking about texts

As an A-level student, you are required to demonstrate an understanding that the meaning of a text is not 'fixed' and that at various places within a text different interpretations are possible. These different interpretations may be supported by reference to the ideas of named critics or particular critical perspectives, but they may also emerge from your own discussions with other students and with your teacher. Either way, what really matters is that you have come to a personal interpretation of the novel through an understanding of the variety of ways in which its meanings are made.

Critical approaches

In 1968 the French literary theorist Roland Barthes wrote a hugely influential essay called *The Death of the Author*, in which he argued that the idea of an author or authority led people to believe it was possible to decode and hence explain the essential 'meaning' of a text. For Barthes, the multiple different ways of making meaning in language and the fact that it is impossible to know the author's state of mind pretty much made a mockery of the idea of a 'knowable text'. The Marxist Barthes saw the concept of the author as another method of transforming a text into a consumer product that could be used up and replaced in a bourgeois westernised capitalist culture.

Building critical skills

As well as Roland Barthes, other critics closely associated with reader-response include the German Wolfgang Iser (1926–2007) and the American Stanley Fish (b. 1938). You might wish to research their ideas online and see how far you think they might be applied to *The Handmaid's Tale* and the other texts you are studying for A-level.

While the 'death of the author' theory might at first seem to suggest Roland Barthes effectively cut the reader's safety rope and left him or her dangling off a literary cliff, in fact his ideas can be seen as heralding the 'birth of the reader' and so empowering him or her. The reader-response approach to literature suggests that writers and readers *collaborate* to make meanings and that our responses will depend upon our own experiences, ideas and values. Unlike literary theories or critical positions that concentrate on the author, content or form of the text, reader-response theory privileges the role of the active reader in creating textual meanings. If you remember this, you may well feel more confident in assessing the performances, interpretations and literary-critical points of view you encounter. Moreover, by setting the novel at the centre of an intertextual web of contexts and connections, you can start to trace the assumptions underlying both *The Handmaid's Tale* itself and the responses of various readers to the text. By resisting the notion of fixed meanings, you are free to make the most of the shifting and unstable nature of the text itself. Thus while this section covers a variety of modern critical approaches that can shed considerable light on the novel, remember that you too are a critic, and as such you should always try to form your own interpretation of the text.

Feminist criticism

Feminist critics are interested in how women are represented in literature and in challenging dominant traditional attitudes and ideas about how female characters (who are often seen through the eyes of male writers) feel, act and think. Feminist criticism challenges patriarchal assumptions by unpicking the gender stereotyping embodied in a text and exploring how such stereotypes can be undermined and resisted.

The Handmaid's Tale is, of course, an iconic text within the canon of women's writing and it is impossible to imagine studying it without applying a feminist critique of some kind. Women characters drive this first-person account by a female narrator and play major roles in the text, while core issues associated with traditional male and female gender roles – such as childbirth, homemaking, education, work and civil rights – are extensively debated within the context of the novel. Relationships between female characters are varied, vividly drawn, interestingly problematic and highly convincing, and male–female relationships are analysed and dissected in forensic detail. Nevertheless, given that *The Handmaid's Tale* was written more than three decades ago, it is worth asking yourself if there are any aspects of the ways in which female characters are represented within it that may now seem dated or stereotyped.

> **CRITICAL VIEW**
>
> In her influential work *The Laugh of the Medusa* (1975), the French feminist critic Hélène Cixous (b. 1937) coined the term *écriture féminine* to articulate what she saw as the challenges women face to find a way of expressing female difference in texts. Her view is that language is not neutral, but forces women writers to communicate in a 'male' voice, not allowing them to truly express themselves; *écriture féminine* theoretically offers a way for women writers to escape this trap.

Political criticism

The German philosopher and political thinker Karl Marx (1818–83) was the founder of modern communism. In *The Communist Manifesto* (1848) Marx stated, 'The history of all hitherto existing society is the history of class struggles.' Thus a Marxist literary critical perspective sees works of literature as inevitably conditioned by and reflective of the economic and political forces of their social context.

Political criticism, which might include historicist and Marxist approaches, reminds us that literary texts are products of a particular set of socio-political circumstances – and that they cannot be divorced from these. Historicists remind us how texts engage with the warp and weft of history and look at the ways in which readers often find in texts ideas that confirm their own. Marxist critics see

Building
critical skills

A historicist view of *The Handmaid's Tale* might stress that explaining how the Gileadean coup was in part triggered by economic and environmental problems reveals Atwood's concerns about the consumerist and materialistic nature of American society in the 1980s.
A Marxist reading of the text might well suggest that human relationships are inevitably warped and distorted by the forces of a capitalist system. How do you respond to these views?

literary texts as material products, which are part of – and help to explain – the processes of history, as Terry Eagleton notes:

> *Marxist criticism is not merely a 'sociology of literature', concerned with how novels get published and whether they mention the working class. Its aim is to explain the literary work more fully; and this means a sensitive attention to its forms, styles and meanings. But it also means grasping those forms, styles and meanings as the product of a particular history.*

(Eagleton, *Marxism and Literary Criticism*, 1976: 2)

Marxist critics see capitalism as a system in which most people work to produce goods and services but do not share equally in the benefits of their labour because the ruling class owns the means of production. Hence Marxist critics see literature as inevitably bound up with the economic and political forces of the times in which it was written. Although not often characterised as an overtly or primarily 'political' writer, Margaret Atwood was still very much engaged with contemporary (i.e. 1980s) American society. For Atwood, a character like Offred, who lacks any social, political and economic authority, is by definition clearly and heavily politicised. The writer's conception of a nightmare system of government, predicated on establishing inequality and unfairness among the people it rules, makes *The Handmaid's Tale* an overtly political text. The narrative constantly exposes and condemns the norms, ideas and values of the Republic of Gilead, together with its laws, religion and system of education. It is certainly possible to view the novel through a Marxist critical lens as being a text about inequality, injustice or oppression, in which the characters' lives are powerfully shaped by the social and economic conditions in which they live. Aspects of the text that would be well worth reviewing through this critical lens include:

- The closure of women's bank accounts and the sacking of women workers after the Gileadean coup.
- The strictly hierarchical social structures within the Gileadean regime.
- The division of the labour force, both male and female.
- The ways in which citizens who are perceived as an economic burden are persecuted, exiled or killed.

Psychoanalytic criticism

Sigmund Freud published one of the founding texts of psychoanalysis, *The Interpretation of Dreams*, in 1900. Psychoanalytic critics see literature as dreamlike, since both fictions and dreams are inventions of the mind that, although based on reality, are obviously not literally true. Psychoanalytic critics look at the significance of the subconscious in order to explore literary representation of character. Working with the theories developed by Freud over a century ago, they analyse the effect of dreams, unconscious desires and aspects of human sexuality, attaching great significance to the underlying hidden meanings of words and actions as revealing the essential truth about someone's state of mind. Several key scenes and events within *The Handmaid's Tale* lend themselves to being viewed through this critical lens, such as:

- **Offred's dream sequences and romance fantasies** might be viewed as regressions to the past or as displacement illusions predicated upon the present being too frightening to be looked at directly.

- **Offred's apparent symptoms of sensory deprivation and synaesthesia.** The ways in which Offred's subjective internal experiences often seem to go against 'normal' rules suggest that seeing the world differently is another of her defence mechanisms. Sensory deprivation (sometimes called perceptual isolation) is when a victim's ability to use one or more of their senses is cut off; this can cause fear, depression and even hallucinations. Offred experiences these kinds of symptoms in response to having what she can see (and often specifically *read*), hear, taste and touch artificially restricted. The term synaesthesia (which is derived from the Greek meaning 'union of the senses') describes a kind of sensory confusion, in which stimulating one sense triggers a response in another, such as being able to smell a colour. Synaesthetes perceive the world differently and, unlike those who suffer sensory deprivation, can find their experiences pleasant. When reading the forbidden letters while playing Scrabble with the Commander, for instance, Offred wants to taste the tiles. 'The counters are like candies, made of peppermint, cool like that. Humbugs, those were called. I would like to put them into my mouth. They would taste also of lime. The letter C. Crisp, slightly acid on the tongue, delicious' (Atwood 1996: 149). Elsewhere she describes feeling like 'the sound of glass. I feel like the word *shatter*' (p.113). Later still, she describes a man's voice as 'metal-coloured, horn-shaped' (p.230).

- **The relationship that develops between Offred and the Commander during their secret meetings** might be likened to a form of capture-bonding sometimes known as Stockholm Syndrome. This phenomenon occurs when prisoners or hostages develop such positive emotional ties to their captors that they may come to identify with them despite being threatened or abused. One attempt to explain this apparently bizarre behaviour uses the theories of Sigmund Freud to argue that emotionally bonding with the captor allows the victim to protect and preserve a sense of their own self-worth and is a defence or survival instinct or strategy used by victims of abuse.

- **The feigned illnesses of the Commanders' Wives**, who often take it in turns to pretend to be sick; Offred thinks their hypochondria makes their empty lives more interesting. Medical experts have long noted how the mind and the body interact and the father of modern psychiatry, Sigmund

Building critical skills

In *The Uses of Enchantment* (1976), Bruno Bettelheim applied a psychological reading to various famous fairy tales, arguing that being exposed to their darker themes of violence, abuse, abandonment and death allows children to externalise their deepest emotional fears and come to terms with them. How far do think that reading dystopian fiction might perform a similar function for adults?

Freud, was very interested in the idea that some illnesses are psychosomatic and stem from psychological rather than physical causes. While the Wives may be faking their physical symptoms, is it possible that their hollow lives are creating very real mental health problems?

Context

Famous victims of apparent Stockholm Syndrome include Patty Hearst, the American heiress held hostage by a gang of revolutionaries who was brainwashed into robbing a bank alongside them, and Natascha Kampusch, the Austrian kidnap victim held prisoner by Wolfgang Priklopil for eight years. Newspaper reports suggest that when told of Priklopil's suicide, Kampusch cried and lit a candle for him. You can read an excellent article by Kathryn Westcott on this phenomenon on the BBC website (a full web address can be found on p.103)

▾ **The nervous breakdowns suffered by Janine/Ofwarren at the Red Centre and after the Particicution**, when she seems to suffer an episode of dissociative fugue. A fugue state is a rare psychiatric condition in which the patient undergoes a severe identity crisis; the disorder is often sparked off by a period of intense physical or emotional stress. At times people may even seek to establish a new identity while in a fugue state, only to then undergo an episode of amnesia. In regressing to her former life as a waitress, this seems to be exactly what Janine is doing.

Queer theory

The term 'queer theory' was coined in 1990, but since the late 1960s, as Julie Rivkin and Michael Ryan note, critics had begun to examine the 'history of the oppression of gays, lesbians, and practitioners of sexualities other than those deemed normal by the dominant heterosexual group', as well as the 'countercultures of gay and lesbian writing that existed in parallel fashion with the dominant heterosexual culture' (Rivkin and Ryan, *Literary Theory*, 1999: 888). Queer theory is grounded in a debate about whether a person's sexuality is part of their essential self or is socially constructed, questioning the default representation of heterosexuality as 'normal' and exploring 'non-heteronormative' sexual behaviour.

The key character to consider here is Moira, whose bravery, humour and daring is celebrated and admired by the narrator. While the Gileadean Republic within the text insists that heterosexuality is 'normal' and homosexuality 'abnormal', going so far as to execute gay men as 'Gender Traitors', the reader is encouraged to celebrate Moira's heroism and defiance. It might be possible to argue that the fact that she plays only a supporting role in the text – albeit a significant one – suggests that positioning a lesbian character as the text's narrative focus was a bridge too far for Atwood. Moira's refusal to become a Handmaid, however, means that she could never have told the story Offred narrates: that of a much more ordinary and much less heroic woman enduring life under the regime. Offred can function as an 'Everywoman' character in a way that Moira never could.

CRITICAL VIEW

Critics closely associated with queer theory include the Americans Eve Kosofsky Sedgwick (1950–2009) and Adrienne Rich (1929–2012). You might wish to research their ideas using the internet and see how far you think their ideas might be applied to *The Handmaid's Tale* and the other texts you are studying for A-level.

Ecocriticism

Ecocriticism is a way of reading texts that involves looking at the ways in which literature treats the subject of nature and the environment. The disaster that has overtaken the former North America and rendered most of its population sterile is left unnamed, but the looming fear of being sent to the Colonies to pick over nuclear waste is a powerful agent of social control within the Gileadean regime. Most people banished there survive for less than three years. This critical lens may well be useful to you when looking at the key environmental messages embedded within *The Handmaid's Tale*.

Assessment Objectives and skills

> **AO1** Articulate informed, personal and creative responses to literary texts, using associated concepts and terminology, and coherent, accurate written expression

To do well with AO1 you need to write fluently, structuring your essay carefully, guiding your reader clearly through your line of argument and using the sophisticated vocabulary, including critical terminology, that is appropriate to an A-level essay. You will need to use frequent embedded quotations to show detailed knowledge and to demonstrate familiarity with the whole text. Your aim is to produce a well-written academic essay employing appropriate discourse markers to create the sense of a shaped argument; it should use sophisticated terminology at times while remaining clear and cohesive.

> **AO2** Analyse ways in which meanings are shaped in literary texts

Strong students do not work only on a lexical level, but also write well on the generic and structural elements of the novel, so it is useful to start by analysing those larger elements of narrative organisation before considering Atwood's language. If 'form is meaning', what are the implications of categorising the text as a postmodern dystopia? *The Handmaid's Tale* is structured in a very distinctive way; think about Atwood's decision to switch between the 'Night' and implied 'Day' sections, for instance. Then again, to discuss language in detail you will need to quote from the novel, analyse that quotation and use it to illuminate your argument. Moreover, since you will at times need to make points about larger generic and organisational features of the text that are much too long to quote in full, being able to reference effectively is just as important as mastering the art of the embedded quotation. Practise writing in analytical sentences, comprising a brief quotation or close reference, a definition or description of the feature you intend to analyse, an explanation of how this feature has been used and an evaluation of its effectiveness.

> **AO3** Demonstrate understanding of the significance and influence of the contexts in which literary texts are written and received

To access AO3 you need to think about how contexts of production, reception, literature, culture, biography, geography, society, history, genre and intertextuality can affect texts. Place the novel at the heart of the web of contextual factors that you feel have had the most impact upon it; examiners want to see a sense of contextual alertness woven seamlessly into the fabric of your essay rather than a clumsy bolted-on website rehash or some recycled class notes. Show you understand that literary works contain encoded representations of the cultural, moral, religious, racial and political values of the society from which they emerged, and that over time attitudes and ideas change until the views they reflect are no longer widely shared.

AO4   Explore connections across literary texts

If your examination board requires you to compare and contrast one or more other texts with *The Handmaid's Tale*, you must try to find specific points of comparison rather than merely generalising. You will find it easier to make connections between texts (of any kind) if you try to balance them as you write; remember also that connections are not only about finding similarities – differences are just as interesting. Above all, consider how the comparison illuminates each text; some connections will be thematic, others generic or stylistic.

AO5   Explore literary texts informed by different interpretations

---

For this AO, you should refer to the opinions of critics and remain alert to those aspects of the novel that are open to interpretation. Your job is to measure your own interpretation of the text against those of other readers. As a text that has generated widely differing responses, *The Handmaid's Tale* lends itself readily to the range of interpretations noted in the 'Critical Contexts' section on pages 78–83. Try to convey an awareness of multiple readings as well as an understanding that (as Barthes suggested) the book's meaning is dependent as much upon what you bring to it as on what Atwood left there. Using modal verb phrases such as 'may be seen as', 'might be interpreted as' or 'could be represented as' shows you understand that different readers will interpret a text in different ways at different times. The key word here is plurality; there is no single meaning or one right answer. Relish getting your teeth into the views of published critics to push forward your own argument, but always keep in mind that meanings in texts are shifting and unstable, as opposed to fixed and permanent.

Summary

Overall, the hallmarks of a successful A-level essay that hits all five AOs include:

- A clear introduction that orientates the reader and outlines your main argument.
- A coherent and conceptualised argument that relates to the question title.
- Confident movement around the text rather than a relentless chronological trawl through it.

◥ Apt and effective quotations or references, adapted to make sense within the context of your own sentence.

◥ A range of effective points about Atwood's narrative methods.

◥ A strong and personally engaged awareness of how a text can be interpreted by different readers and audiences in different ways at different times.

◥ A sense that you are prepared to take on a good range of critical and theoretical perspectives.

◥ A conclusion that effectively summarises and consolidates your response and relates it back to your essay title.

Building skills 1: Structuring your writing

This section focuses on organising your written responses to convey your ideas as clearly and effectively as possible: the 'how' of your writing as opposed to the 'what'. More often than not, if your knowledge and understanding of *The Handmaid's Tale* is sound, a disappointing mark or grade will be down to one of two common mistakes: misreading the question or failing to organise your response economically and effectively. In an examination you'll be lucky if you can demonstrate 5 per cent of what you know about *The Handmaid's Tale*; fortunately, if it's the right 5 per cent, that's all you need to gain full marks.

Understanding your examination

It's important to prepare for the specific type of response your examination body sets with regard to *The Handmaid's Tale*. You'll almost certainly know whether you are studying the novel as part of a **non-examined assessment unit** (i.e. for coursework) or as an **examination set text**. If it's the latter you also need to know if your paper is **open book**, i.e. you will have a clean copy of the text available to you in the exam, or **closed book**, in which case you won't. You really need to find out about this, because the format of your assessment has major implications for the way you organise your response and dictates the depth and detail required to achieve a top band mark.

Open book

In an open book exam, when you have a copy of *The Handmaid's Tale* on the desk in front of you, there can be no possible excuse for failing to quote relevantly, accurately and extensively. To gain a high mark, you are expected to focus in detail on specific passages. Remember, too, that you must not refer to any supporting material such as a scholarly introduction or set of notes contained within your copy of the text. If an examiner suspects that you have been lifting chunks of unacknowledged material from such a source, they will refer your paper to the examining body for possible malpractice.

Closed book

In a closed book exam, because the examiner is well aware that you do not have the text in front of you, their expectations will be different. You are still expected to support your argument with relevant quotations, and close textual references are also encouraged and rewarded. Since you will have had to memorise quotations, slight inaccuracies will not be severely punished. Rather than a forensically detailed analysis of a specific section of *The Handmaid's Tale*, the examiner will expect you to range more broadly across the book to structure your response.

Non-examined assessment

Writing about *The Handmaid's Tale* within a non-examined assessment (NEA) unit (i.e. coursework) context poses a very different set of challenges from an examination, in that incorrect quotations and disorientating arguments are liable to cost you much more dearly. Your essay must be wholly and consistently relevant to the title selected; there's no excuse for going off track if you or your teacher mapped out the parameters of your chosen topic in the first place.

Step 1: Planning and beginning: locate the debate

A very common type of exam question invites you to open up a debate about the text by using various trigger words and phrases, such as **'Consider the view that…'**, **'Some readers think that…'** or **'How far do you agree that…?'** When analysing this type of question, the one thing you can be sure of is that exam questions never offer a view that makes no sense at all or one so blindingly obvious that all anyone can do is agree with it; there will always be a genuine interpretation at stake. Similarly, many NEA tasks are written to include a stated view to help give some shape to your writing, so logically your introduction needs to orientate the reader by addressing the terms of this debate and sketching out the outline of how you intend to move the argument forward. Since it's obviously going to be helpful if you actually know this before you start writing, you really do need to plan before you begin to write.

Undertaking a lively debate about some of the ways in which *The Handmaid's Tale* has been and can be interpreted is the DNA of your essay. Of course, any good argument needs to be honest; to begin by writing 'Yes, I totally agree with this obviously true statement' suggests a fundamental misunderstanding of what studying literature is all about. The given views in examination questions are designed to open up critical conversations, not to shut them down.

Plan your answer by collecting together points for and against the given view. Aim to see a stated opinion as an interesting way of focusing upon a key facet of *The Handmaid's Tale*, like the following student.

Student A

This student is answering a sample examination task from AQA Specification B that works with a given view. The question, which is clearly designed to open up a debate, is:

'*The Handmaid's Tale* is not primarily about the suppression of women but about their defiance.' To what extent do you agree with this view?

Remember to include relevant detailed exploration of Atwood's authorial methods in your answer.

*To some extent I would argue that The Handmaid's Tale may be seen as about **both** the suppression of women within the*

Gileadean theocracy **as well as** their defiance, since it is in response to the ingrained sexism of the patriarchal regime that some women eventually revolt. Apart from the bullied and intimidated Janine, who is renamed Ofwarren, all the major female characters defy the authorities to some extent — even the Commander's Wife, Serena Joy, who would seem to be so privileged that she has no reason to rebel. Interestingly it is not the central character and first-person narrator Offred who is the most defiant woman in the text, but her best friend Moira, who refuses to become a Handmaid and prefers to work as a prostitute at Jezebel's. Because she is a lesbian, the strong-willed Moira is seen as a dangerous Unwoman; significantly she is always given her own name, unlike the official Handmaids.

Atwood structures the text to contrast Offred's past and present and uses this technique to draw the reader's attention to the difference between suppressed and defiant women. One of Offred's crucial flashbacks takes her back in time to an incident at the Red Centre involving the polarised characters of Moira and Janine. Whereas Moira escaped from the Aunts' attempts to brainwash and suppress her, Janine was mentally broken by the process, admitting that it was her fault that she was gang-raped as a teenager and exhibiting unmistakable signs of a psychological illness that seems rather like PTSD.

Atwood directly contrasts Janine's breakdown, where she regresses to her past life as a waitress, mechanically repeating phrases such as 'You have a nice day now', with Moira's almost violent response; Moira actually slaps her across the face, 'twice, back and forth'. Atwood suggests here that Moira is only too well aware that unless you keep defying authority and carve out a pathway on your own terms, in Gilead you will go under. This is why she tells Offred, 'You can't let her go slipping over the edge. That stuff is catching.' To the bitter end, Moira remains defiant, managing a thrilling escape from the Red Centre that involves taking one of the Aunts hostage and threatening to stab her to death before deciding to take her chances as a Jezebel until she is exiled to the Colonies. For Offred (and also the reader) Moira is a role model and the true heroine of the novel. When Offred meets Moira at Jezebel's, wearing a demeaning Playboy Bunny outfit, she is initially disappointed. 'I don't want her to be like me', says Offred. 'Give in, go along, save her skin.' Yet Moira reassures Offred, explaining that she has deliberately chosen this fate. Paradoxically, becoming a Jezebel is Moira's final insult to the Gileadean authorities, a calculated gesture indicating her absolute determination to defy them and refuse to have her spirit suppressed like Janine.

Examiner's commentary

This student:

- ▼ Deftly takes on the central premise of the question from the outset.
- ▼ Expresses a confident and original personal view.
- ▼ Keeps returning to the question's key terms: 'defiance' (which sometimes becomes 'defiant' or 'defy') and 'suppression'.
- ▼ Deals with some key features of AO2 in terms of Atwood's narrative structure and use of Moira and Janine as foils.
- ▼ Creates a convincing, fluent and well-supported argument that Moira and Janine can be seen to represent defiance and suppression, respectively.
- ▼ Quotes frequently and appositely, ranging across the text well to select the most useful short phrases to support the argument.
- ▼ Advances the original and interesting idea that Janine may be seen as suffering from PTSD (post-traumatic stress disorder) due to her terrible experiences in Gilead.

If the rest of this essay reached this level of performance, it is likely this student would be on course to achieve a notional grade A.

Step 2: Developing and linking: go with the flow

An essay is a very specific type of formal writing that requires an appropriate discourse structure. In the main body of your writing, you need to thread your developing argument through each paragraph consistently and logically, referring back to the terms established by the question itself, rephrasing and reframing as you go. It can be challenging to sustain the flow of your essay and keep firmly on track, but here are some techniques to help you:

- ▼ Ensure your essay doesn't disintegrate into a series of disconnected blobs by creating a stable bridge between one paragraph and the next.
- ▼ Use discourse markers – linking words and phrases like 'on the other hand', 'however', 'although' and 'moreover' – to hold the individual paragraphs of your essay together and to signpost the connections between different sections of your overarching argument.

- Having set out an idea in Paragraph A, in Paragraph B you might need to then back it up by providing a further example; if so, signal this to your reader with a phrase such as *'**Moreover**, this defiance can also be seen when…'*
- To change direction and challenge an idea begun in Paragraph A by acknowledging that it is open to interpretation, you could begin Paragraph B with something like *'**On the other hand**, this view of the text could be challenged by a feminist critic…'*
- Another typical paragraph-to-paragraph link is when you want to show that the original idea doesn't give the full picture. Here you could modify your original point with something like *'**Although** it is possible to see Offred as not just less defiant than both Ofglen and Moira but actually very passive once she has begun her love affair with Nick, this view does not take account of the fact that bearing witness to the truth about Gilead is in itself a clear act of defiance.'*

Step 3: Concluding: seal the deal

As you bring your writing to a close, you need to capture and clarify your response to the given view and make a relatively swift and elegant exit. Keep your final paragraph short and sweet. Now is not the time to introduce any new points – but equally, don't just reword everything you have already said either. Neat potential closers include:

- Looping the last paragraph back to something you mentioned in your introduction to suggest that you have now said all you have to say on the subject.
- Reflecting on your key points in order to reach a balanced overview.
- Ending with a punchy quotation that leaves the reader thinking.
- Discussing the contextual implications of the topic you have debated.
- Reversing expectations to end on an interesting alternative view.
- Stating why you think the main issue, theme or character under discussion is so central to the novel.
- Mentioning how different audiences over time might have responded to the topic you have been debating.

Student B

This is the conclusion of another student's essay, answering the same question as Student A:

'*The Handmaid's Tale* is not primarily about the suppression of women but about their defiance.' To what extent do you agree with this view?

Remember to include relevant detailed exploration of Atwood's authorial methods in your answer.

To conclude, I think that yes, The Handmaid's Tale is mainly but not totally about women being suppressed. Most obviously the character of Janine (Ofwarren) shows this, but even Serena Joy is oppressed, which is ironic given that she worked to set up the conservative values of Gilead in her former life. Although Offred commits small acts of defiance like stealing Serena Joy's daffodil, before going behind her back to have an affair with Commander Fred, it is really Moira who is the rebel. The flashback to the Red Centre and the contrast between Moira and Janine show this clearly. Therefore I agree to a large extent that the novel is mostly about the suppression of women and not defiance, since hardly any women rebel successfully.

Examiner's commentary

This student:

- Tries to signal that she is concluding a debate about the central premise of the question.
- Does return to the question's key terms: 'defiance' and 'suppression'.
- Touches on a key feature of AO2 in terms of Atwood's use of Moira and Janine as foils, but does not clinch the point.
- Does not quote from the text, but includes a clear and relevant reference to Offred's theft of Serena Joy's flower to support her argument.

If the previous sections of this essay had been of a similar quality, it is likely this student would be on course to achieve a notional grade C.

Building skills 2: Analysing texts in detail

Having worked through the previous section on structuring your writing, this section of the guide contains two more extracts from students' responses to *The Handmaid's Tale*. The next few pages will enable you to assess the extent to which these students have successfully demonstrated their writing skills and mastery of the Assessment Objectives, to provide you with an index by which to measure the progress of your own skills. Both extracts come with a commentary to help you identify what each student is doing well and/or what changes they would need to make to their writing in order to target a higher grade.

The main focus here is on the ways in which you can successfully include within your own well-structured writing clear and appropriate references to both *The Handmaid's Tale* itself and the ways in which other readers have responded to the novel. In an examination, of course, the 'other reading' you need to refer to consistently is encoded within the question itself: the 'given view', in other words. In a non-examined assessment unit, you will have more choice about which interpretations of the text you most want to work with – but since you have much more time and may well have written your own question title, you have even less excuse to wander off task.

Student C

This student is answering a sample examination task from AQA Specification A that works with a given view. The question, which is clearly designed to open up a debate, is:

'In Gilead, men are victims too.'

Examine this view of Atwood's presentation of male characters in *The Handmaid's Tale*.

Although The Handmaid's Tale is usually interpreted as a feminist text, Margaret Atwood does not paint all men as bad and all women as good. I would argue that in the novel she definitely presents men as victims as well as oppressors; Luke, Nick and even the Commander himself suffer under the regime. In some ways these three most significant male characters are trapped by the strict Gileadean codes of behaviour every bit as tightly as the women are. Although the text focuses on the terrible experiences of women such as Offred, Ofglen, Moira and Janine, most of which are the direct result of patriarchal attitudes and male oppression, Atwood's descriptions of the Wall, the Particicution and the fate of Gender Traitors shows that Gilead oppresses all its citizens, male and female. It is true to say, however, that the strict gender roles that are enforced in the republic mean that men and women are victimised in very different ways.

The rigid hierarchy of the state means that those at the top, like the Commander, have access to a whole range of privileges forbidden to men of lower status like Nick, who is only a Guardian. The Commander – who was one of the Sons of Jacob who made up the sexist rules of the new society and may well have been responsible for designing the robes that identify the different types of women – has a Wife, two Marthas and a Handmaid. He has a chauffeur, an expensive car, and access to all the good things that Gilead affords. Yet Atwood suggests that even he suffers under the restrictions imposed by the theocracy, secretly rebelling against rules whenever he can, playing Scrabble with Offred, allowing her to read magazines in his study and, most of all, dressing her up as an 'evening rental' to take her out to Jezebel's. The Commander, who Offred knows is 'not an unkind man', reveals his basic vulnerability when he seems desperate to know that Offred likes him for himself when they have sex in the hotel room; 'I thought you might enjoy it for a change,' he says. Paradoxically, however, he has helped to set up a system that wrecks normal human relationships, and so he remains 'dismayed and no doubt disappointed' as Offred tries to 'fake it'. In juxtaposing this awkward and embarrassing 'love scene' with Offred's growing passion for Nick, we see that by conveniently ignoring 'love', the Commander has ensured that he can never have what he most desires.

It is interesting to note that while Offred eventually escapes at the end of the novel, managing to get away and record her narrative on to some old cassette tapes, the Commander himself is not so lucky. There is a clear hint in the final scene that he is suspected of the 'Violation of state secrets' and his gesture of putting 'his hands to his head' reveals his terror and apprehension. Paranoid as to which one of his enemies has stabbed him in the back, Atwood does seem to portray him as a victim at this point, and since it is the last time we see him, this leaves a powerful final impression. As Offred notices on her way out of his house, 'I am above him, looking down; he is shrinking. There have already been purges among them, there will be more.' Moreover, in the postmodern Historical Notes section that closes the novel, Atwood seems to validate Offred's theory when Professor Pieixoto suggests that Commander Fred might be 'Frederick R. Waterford', who was eventually purged for having 'liberal tendencies'.

Examiner's commentary

This student:

◥ Realises that the focus of his essay must be on the male characters, and does not try to twist the question by implying that the given view is completely wrong in order to write about the female characters instead.

◥ Mentions Margaret Atwood as the maker of textual meaning frequently when analysing her methods and themes.

◥ Forges a very clear link between his paragraphs that reassures the examiner that he is still fully on task.

◥ Uses phrase such as 'usually interpreted as a feminist text' and 'I would argue', together with the subtle verb 'seems', to flag up his awareness that textual meanings are not fixed and are always open to question.

◥ Embeds short, relevant quotations seamlessly within his own sentences, so that the flow of his writing is not disrupted.

◥ Quotes frequently and always relevantly – just a couple of well-chosen words being enough at times, such as when he quotes Offred's decision to '**fake it**' or mentions the Commander's 'liberal tendencies'.

If the rest of this examination answer reached this level of performance, it is likely this student would be on course to achieve a notional grade A.

Top ten quotation

Student D

This student is answering a sample examination task from AQA Specification A that works with a given view. The question, which is clearly designed to open up a debate, is:

Examine the view that, in *The Handmaid's Tale*, Atwood's primary concern is sexual violence against women.

I strongly agree that the theme of sexual violence against women is the main point of the book, mainly because of Offred getting raped by the Commander during the Ceremony. Men do not experience sexual attacks like women do as Gilead is such a sexist society. During the Ceremony Offred has shocking taboo language, 'what he is fucking is the lower half of my body', and this shows she hates that he gets to use her like this simply because she is only a Handmaid and the state allows this. She says the Handmaids are only 'two-legged wombs' which makes them seem subhuman and only there to provide babies through being raped, or at any rate forced to submit to sex, with powerful men. There is also the story of how Janine was gang-raped and ended up blaming herself for it after Aunt

Lydia brainwashed her. The way that the Jezebels, especially Moira, are forced to work in a brothel can be seen as another example of sexual violence against women. Atwood is also concerned about explaining how pornography created a situation where violence against women grew worse until there was the revolution against the USA government.

Top ten quotation

Examiner's commentary

Note how this student:

◥ Fails to really analyse the terms of the given view that Atwood's primary concern is sexual violence against women, i.e. whether it is fair to say it is the essential or overriding concern of the text.

◥ Makes the central premise of the question central to her argument but does not sustain a sense of really debating the interpretation stated.

◥ Refers to useful and relevant parts of the text.

◥ Uses a potentially helpful direct quotation but without fully analysing its effects.

◥ Tries to address AO2 by writing about taboo language and using the useful reference to '**two-legged wombs**'.

◥ Makes some statements that are very much open to question, or at the very least require further explanation. Describing Offred's sexual relationship with the Commander as 'rape' is clearly wrong; during her description of the Ceremony in Chapter 16, she explicitly states 'nor does rape cover it; nothing is going on here that I haven't signed up for. There wasn't a lot of choice but there was some, and this is what I chose' (Atwood 1996: 105). Again, Moira *chooses* to work at Jezebel's in preference to being sent to the colonies as an Unwoman. The mention of the horrific gang-rape of Janine is potentially more promising as it is a clear and highly relevant example of sexual violence against women within the text, but it lacks textual support and remains unanalysed.

If the rest of this examination answer reached this rather uneven level of performance, it is likely this student would be on course to achieve a notional low grade C.

Before studying this section, you should identify your own 'top ten' quotations – i.e. those phrases or sentences that seem to capture a key theme or aspect of the text most aptly and memorably – and clearly identify what it is about your choices that makes each one so significant. No two readers of *The Handmaid's Tale* will select exactly the same set and it will be well worth discussing (and perhaps even having to defend) your choices with the other students in your class.

When you have done this, look carefully at the following list of top ten quotations and consider each one's possible significance within the novel. How might each be used in an essay response to support your exploration of various elements or readings of *The Handmaid's Tale*? Consider what these quotations tell us about Margaret Atwood's ideas, themes and methods, as well as how far they may contribute to various potential ways of interpreting the text.

'We were the people who were not in the papers. We lived in the blank white spaces at the edges of print.' (p.66)

1

▼ Offred reflects on her life before the Gileadean revolution as an ordinary woman whose life was never exciting or unusual enough to leave a permanent record. Now that newspapers are forbidden artefacts associated with the crime of reading, her point emphasises the invisibility of women within the context of the theocracy. With print having failed her, she has recourse to speech to tell her story, recording her voice on to a set of old cassette tapes.

'I wait. I compose myself. My self is a thing I must now compose, as one composes a speech. What I must present is a made thing, not something born.' (p.76)

2

▼ Here, Offred plays with the two meanings of the verb 'to compose', i.e. 'to calm oneself' and 'to create a work of art'. On one level she needs to prepare herself with composure to undergo the Ceremony, during which she will participate in a surreal three-way sexual encounter with the Commander and Serena Joy. Underneath this, though, she must find a way of presenting an unreal doppelgänger fashioned purely to endure this bizarre ordeal. Thus the quotation suggests the presence of two women, the 'made thing' she has faked in order to survive the Ceremony and the real Offred who is 'something born'. In addition, these lines draw attention to the narrator's conscious awareness that she is telling a story; she speaks of herself as being like a text in some ways – or at least a **palimpsest** that has been

A **palimpsest** is a piece of text in which, although the original writing has been wiped out, overwritten and altered, traces of the earlier writing remain.

deliberately overwritten. We might also see a reflection of the famous French feminist philosopher Simone de Beauvoir's contention that 'one is not born, but becomes, a woman'.

Context

In *The Second Sex* (1949), Simone de Beauvoir analysed the treatment of women throughout history. This text is often seen as a core work of feminist philosophy. Its relevance to *The Handmaid's Tale* is clear.

3 'We are for breeding purposes: we aren't concubines, geisha girls, courtesans … no room is to be permitted for the flowering of secret lusts; no special favours are to be wheedled, by them or us, there are to be no toeholds for love. We are two-legged wombs, that's all: sacred vessels, ambulatory chalices.' (p.146)

▼ Offred analyses the nature of her role in Commander Fred's life on the night she makes her first secret and forbidden visit to his study. She describes herself as falling outside the category of mistress or desirable 'other woman', and the nouns 'vessel' and 'chalice' stress that it would be the child inside her that mattered, not the woman who carried it. Here, three types of women whose recognised roles are highly sexualised are juxtaposed with the holy purity of the religious iconography, stressing how in Gilead sexual pleasure and motherhood have become utterly severed. Offred describes herself as virtually an incarnation of the Virgin Mary, insignificant other than for the child she could carry.

4 'Context is all.' (p.154)

▼ This key phrase is, significantly, presented within its own micro-paragraph. Playing Scrabble with Commander Fred makes Offred realise how everything changes when mapped on to a different time, place or set of circumstances. In pre-Gileadean days, Scrabble might have seemed like a dull board game for old people; in a world where women are forbidden to read, however, it carries an unmistakable sexual charge, as illicit as if they were taking drugs.

'*Nolite te bastardes carborundorum*. I can't see it in the dark but I trace the tiny scratched writing with the ends of my fingers, as if it's a code in Braille. It sounds in my head now less like a prayer, more like a command; but to do what?' (p.156)

5

* The mock-Latin motto of the former Offred – *don't let the bastards grind you down* – becomes a mantra for the narrator; even though for a long time she does not understand its literal meaning. She murmurs it to herself as a prayer before undergoing the ordeal of the Ceremony, well before Commander Fred finally translates it for her. Her predecessor's words transform the phrase into a talismanic chant that enables Offred to channel the spirit of her doppelgänger at key moments. As the narrator grows increasingly rebellious, the phrase transmutes from a prayer into an exhortation and reminder never to submit; for both the Offreds, as Chapter 46 makes clear, suicide is preferable to being captured and exiled by the regime.

"Nature demands variety for men … it's part of the procreational strategy. It's Nature's plan … Women know that instinctively. Why did they buy so many different clothes, in the old days? To trick the men into thinking they were several different women. A new one each day." (p.249)

6

* Commander Fred's comment sums up his lazy and convenient assumption – or is it mere wishful thinking? – that men naturally are meant to want more than one woman, whereas women are (presumably) designed to be faithful to one partner only. This breathtaking hypocrisy shows how, while the men of Gilead draw on biblical precedent to justify their system of arranged marriages and concubinage, they are equally happy to refer to a hazy belief in biological determinism as and when it suits them. The essential incompatibility of these two ideologies suggests the fundamentally misogynist nature of the theocracy. Moreover, his obsessive interest in female clothing and its symbolism is once again revealed.

'Fake it, I scream at myself inside my head. You must remember how. Let's get this over with or you'll be here all night. Bestir yourself. Move your flesh around, breathe audibly. It's the least you can do.' (p.267)

7

* Offred's inability to make love to Commander Fred as if she means it sums up the tragic farce of their relationship. As one of the elite Sons of Jacob who codified and systematised the rules of the theocracy, Commander Fred decided to dispense with love in favour of arranged marriage and concubinage – yet even he finds it impossible to abide by the strict regulations he helped to establish. Officially he is allowed only to have sex with Offred within the confines of the Ceremony, yet these mechanical and loveless encounters offer him

little pleasure. The supreme irony of this episode is that, having been forced into having Ceremonial sex, Offred is incapable of responding to him in any other way; in fact she finds this incident in some ways more futile and depressing than ever. The Commander has helped to ensure that what he most wants – an honest relationship with a woman who likes him for himself – can never happen.

8

'I made that up. It didn't happen that way. Here is what happened.' (p.273)

⌐ Offred's admission that she is recasting the account of her first night with Nick draws attention to the importance of telling stories within The Handmaid's Tale as well as to the novel's status as a postmodern text. In positioning her as a self-confessed unreliable narrator, however, Atwood paradoxically increases the reader's belief that we can depend upon her essential truthfulness. While some details may be blurred, overall, Offred's narrative conveys an unassailable sense of authenticity.

9

'And so I step up, into the darkness within; or else the light.' (p.307)

⌐ The last line of Offred's narrative captures something of the postmodern brilliance of the text, with the tale, like the Handmaid herself, left frozen in time, poised between captivity and freedom. If this were the last line of the whole text, the ending would be totally open and unfixed; as it is, Professor Pieixoto's Historical Notes suggest that she reaches the light at last.

10

'Are there any questions?' (p.324)

⌐ The last line of the whole text is Professor Pieixoto's closing question to the academic conference audience he has been lecturing. It summarises the Professor's belief that he has fleshed out the context as far as he can, that he has said more or less all there is to say about the worth of Offred's narrative as a historical document. Moreover, it draws attention to his rather supercilious conviction that he has decoded and critiqued 'the handmaid's tale' in a thorough and academically rigorous manner. Yet in posing a question rather than providing an answer, how can the reader be sure that Offred's story has really been 'closed'? The Professor is closing his keynote address, but many questions remain unanswered. 'Are there any questions?' invites the reader to respond with 'Yes – several. What was Offred's real name? Did she resume her relationship with Nick? Did she ever see her child again? What happened to Moira? How did the Republic fall?' Thus, in a final postmodern twist, Atwood refuses to tell us any more, and that is, of course, just as it should be. It is left open for the reader to ponder and consider the possibilities.

Books

Atwood, M. (1985) *The Handmaid's Tale* **(1996 edition, Vintage)**

– All references within this study guide are to this standard edition of the text.

Atwood, M. (2005) *Writing with Intent: Essays, Reviews, Personal Prose 1983–2005* **(Carroll and Graf)**

– A fascinating compilation of Atwood's non-fiction, including 'George Orwell: Some personal connections' and 'Writing Utopia'. Includes a discussion of her response to Orwell's dystopian writing as well as the challenges and pleasures of working within the dystopian genre.

Bloom, H. (ed.) (2001) *Margaret Atwood's* **The Handmaid's Tale (Chelsea House Publishers)**

– A scholarly collection of articles on a diverse range of the novel's themes and ideas.

Howells, C.A. (1976) *Margaret Atwood* **(2005 Second Edition, Palgrave Macmillan)**

– A clear and sensitive general overview of Atwood's works.

Howells, C.A. (ed.) (2006) *The Cambridge Companion to Margaret Atwood* **(Cambridge University Press)**

– A superb, wide-ranging and thought-provoking collection of scholarly articles.

Macpherson, H.S. (2010) *The Cambridge Introduction to Margaret Atwood* **(Cambridge University Press)**

– An excellent and accessible summary of the Atwood canon.

Nischik, R.M. (ed.) (2000) *Margaret Atwood: Works and Impact* **(Camden House)**

– A collection of interesting scholarly essays on various aspects of Atwood's novels; several are rather challenging. Particularly worthwhile are:

- 'Transgressing genre: A generic approach to Margaret Atwood's novels' by Coral Ann Howells.
- 'Recycling culture: Kitsch, camp and trash in Atwood's fiction' by Lorna Irvine.
- 'Creativity: An interview with Margaret Atwood' by Gabriele Metzler.
- '"Trust me": Reading the romance plot in Margaret Atwood's *The Handmaid's Tale*' by Madonne Miner.
- 'Narrative games and gender politics' by Barbara Hill Rigney.

Rigney, B.H. (1987) *Women Writers: Margaret Atwood* **(Macmillan Education)**

– Written soon after the publication of *The Handmaid's Tale*, this is a useful overview of Atwood's earlier fiction.

Wisker, G. (2010) *Atwood's* **The Handmaid's Tale**: *A Reader's* **Guide (Continuum)**

– A helpful and accessible guide to the text, which includes some thought-provoking questions to promote class discussion.

Articles

Atwood, M. (2005) 'Aliens have taken the place of Angels: Margaret Atwood on why we need science fiction' in the *Guardian*

www.theguardian.com/film/2005/jun/17/sciencefictionfantasyandhorror. margaretatwood

– A fascinating short essay by the novelist that reveals her ideas about the sci-fi genre. (Accessed July 2015.)

Atwood, M. (2012) 'Rachel Carson's *Silent Spring* **50 years on' in the** *Guardian*

www.theguardian.com/books/2012/dec/07/why-rachel-carson-is-a-saint

– Margaret Atwood considers the impact and legacy of Carson's pioneering environmental work, half a century after it was first published. (Accessed July 2015.)

Flood, A. (2014) 'Margaret Atwood's new work will remain unseen for a century' in the *Guardian*

www.theguardian.com/books/2014/sep/05/margaret-atwood-new-work-unseen-century-future-library

– An overview of the Future Library Project, to which Margaret Atwood is the first contributor. (Accessed July 2015.)

Hoby, H. (2013) 'An interview with Margaret Atwood' in *The Telegraph*

www.telegraph.co.uk/culture/books/10246937/Margaret-Atwood-interview.html

– An interesting interview with the writer that dates from the time her dystopian novel *MaddAddam* was published. (Accessed July 2015.)

Rothstein, M. (1986) 'No balm in Gilead' in *The New York Times*

www.nytimes.com/books/00/09/03/specials/atwood-gilead.html

– In this interview with Mervyn Rothstein, published soon after *The Handmaid's Tale* was released, Margaret Atwood makes it plain that Offred does indeed escape at the end of the novel. (Accessed July 2015.)

Mills, N. (2013) 'Gloria Steinem's 'a bunny's tale' – 50 years later' in
The Guardian

Gloria Steinem's journalistic exposé:
www.theguardian.com/commentisfree/2013/may/26/gloria-steinem-bunny-tale-still-relevant-today

Westcott, K. (2013) 'What is Stockholm syndrome?' in *BBC news online*

Kathryn Westcott's article on Stockholm Syndrome:
www.bbc.co.uk/news/magazine-22447726

Podcasts

BBC Radio 4's World Book Club

www.bbc.co.uk/programmes/p02r76k2

– In this interview with Harriett Gilbert, Margaret Atwood discusses *The Handmaid's Tale* in the presence of a live audience. (Accessed July 2015.)

Film

The Handmaid's Tale (1990)
– Directed by Volker Schlondorff and starring Natasha Richardson as Offred, Robert Duvall as the Commander and Faye Dunaway as Serena Joy, this is a beautiful adaptation with some powerful individual performances. It plays fast and loose with the plotline of the novel, however, and struggles to convey the complexity of the text.